CHRISTIANS IN A WORLD AT WAR

CHRISTIANS IN A WORLD AT WAR

BY

EDWYN BEVAN

STUDENT CHRISTIAN MOVEMENT PRESS
58 BLOOMSBURY STREET, LONDON, W.C.1

First published May 1940

Distributed in Canada by our exclusive agents,
The Macmillan Company of Canada Ltd.,
70 Bond Street, Toronto

PRINTED IN GREAT BRITAIN BY
NORTHUMBERLAND PRESS LIMITED
GATESHEAD ON TYNE

I inscribe this book to the memory of one who was prominent among the leaders of the Student Christian Movement in a generation now grown old, and who, when still young, was struck by a German bullet in the night of May 11, 1915, while trying to answer a wounded man's cry for help,

LESLIE JOHNSTON

my friend, ever-living with God.

And I said, This is my infirmity,
  That the right hand of the Most High should change!

. . . .

Thy way is in the sea,
  And thy paths in the great waters,
  And thy footsteps are not known.

PSALM LXXVII. 10, 19

Jehovah speaks:
When I find the set time,
  I will judge uprightly.
Though the earth and all its inhabitants be dissolved,
  I hold up the pillars of it.

PSALM LXXV. 2, 3

I look for the Resurrection of the dead, and the Life of the World to come.

NICENE CREED

CONTENTS

CHAPTER I

THE UNREALIZED HOPE

When the quiet process of things is brought to a violent interruption, a second time in our generation, by a great war, it is not only the immediate problems which weigh upon the minds of men. They ask whether the world process as a whole into which they are launched at birth has any meaning or purpose or goal, when it allows the occurrence of these shattering catastrophes that confound high-built hopes and show a vast power of destruction granted to the evil will. The event of to-day has its significance from its coming at this moment of a world process, from all the past that led up to it, from all the possibilities of the future. We have that past and future in mind, when we gaze at this conflict of world powers which marks the opening of the nineteen hundred and fortieth year of Grace. In this little volume an attempt is made to see the conflict in its setting, so far as that is constituted by the obstinate hope which has characterized, throughout these nineteen centuries, the view taken in the Christian Church of earthly events. An attempt—because to the matter of these pages the term "essay," so often used of occasional papers, might be applied in the most literal sense.

Nineteen hundred years ago a little body of men were gathered somewhere in the land we know as Palestine. They looked up at the sky and spoke, as if to Some One who was up there beyond the blue expanse. They called Him "Father" and they asked that His Kingdom might come and His will might be done on earth, just as it was done in that other world up there out of sight. This world, as they saw it around them, was a hard, oppressive world. The nation to which they belonged had been chosen, they believed, by God from among all nations to know more than others of His character and purpose and to be a light to the Gentiles. And now it was to those other nations that the kingdom, the power and the glory belonged. Their armies carried their idolatrous standards wherever they would through the land of Israel. Their proconsuls and procurators issued the orders which Israel had to obey. Israel was a subject people under the yoke of the rulers of this world. And in all the lands, near and far, as far as their knowledge reached over the face of the earth, the scattered members of the holy people were subject to the yoke; Gentile emperors and kings bore rule over them. And yet they believed that He who was there above the sky, He before whom all nations were as nothing, as a drop of the bucket, as the small dust of the balance, He who brought princes to nothing and made the judges of the earth as vanity, was in a special way Israel's God, the God of Abraham, Isaac and Jacob. They really believed that! Nevertheless the processes of the iron world went on, grinding the people of His choice, and He did nothing to arrest them, to deflect them. It was just as if He did not exist at all, or had forgotten. The men of the nations could ask them mockingly where this God of theirs, who did nothing at all, was. "Where is now thy God?" All you could see was the processes of the iron world, going on always unchanging, remorselessly, invincibly, irresistibly.

Yet all the time close to this world was the wonder-world of God's glory and power. Yes, there it was, they believed, though you could not see it. Occasionally, old stories said, men had been able for a moment to look into it, or it had broken, abruptly, into the course of things in this world, into the seemingly unchangeable processes, and had changed them. Once, it was told, a prophet's servant had been granted a moment of vision, and had seen, above the host of earthly enemies, the whole air full of horses and chariots of fire round about the prophet.[1] And at other times the powers of that unseen world had intervened in the processes of this world: the waters of the sea or of a river had suddenly rolled back and stood up in a wall to make a passage for the elect people, the sun had stood still in the sky, fire had broken out without earthly cause, dead men had come to life again. According to the ordinary processes of this world, a large, well-equipped army was certain to get the better of a small, poorly armed body of men; but when the powers of the wonder-world came into operation, there was no such certainty: God could save by few, as well as by many. A thousand might flee at the rebuke of one.

Only it was long ago that such things had happened —in the days which the old stories called to mind. Till a few years ago there had seemed to this little group to be no such intervention of the wonder-world in the hard processes of their own time. God seemed now to be always on the side of the big battalions. No fire from heaven blasted the heathen conqueror when he entered into the Holy of Holies; no angel went forth and smote a camp of the Romans, "so that when men arose early in the morning, behold they were all dead corpses."[2] Of course the Jews of

[1] 2 Kings vi. 17. [2] 2 Kings xix. 35.

that time had no such precise notion of the uniformity of natural law as we have to-day. But in a general way everyone must always have distinguished the normal processes of nature from strange exceptions appearing to be the intervention of some Power from a world beyond. And if anyone believes in the existence of such a Power and identifies it with a God whose will is only for good, who cares for righteousness and loves His human children, he must have been sometimes depressed at the way the processes of nature go on in unrelaxing uniformity, without any relation, it would appear, to the conservation of good, everything of spiritual value, every heroic or beautiful personality, every aspiration and achievement, annihilated, sooner or later, by death. The individual, the race, the globe itself may put up for some space of time a fight against death; but death is sure to win in the end, all along the line. Man finds himself imprisoned in these processes: no escape from their iron rules. If only there could be a break in it somewhere to set him free, to save him, to save what he values, from death! It was the absence of such a break in the processes of the world which must have weighed upon the spirits of men in Palestine nineteen hundred years ago, as it has weighed upon the spirits of many men in other countries since.

It is true that the pious in Israel in those days, though they might think it strange and depressing that the wonder-world in which they believed showed no longer any signs of itself and let the processes of this world go on without interference, nevertheless clung to the conviction that this obscuring of the wonder-world was only for a time. Some day it would break in again as it had done of old. It would break in with far greater manifestation of power than of old. All the processes of the world, now so dominant, in all lands inhabited by man, would be arrested and changed by it. All the pride of the heathen empires would vanish in a moment like smoke. Things impossible now in the adaptation of conditions on earth to the happiness and well-being of man would become experienced fact. The glory of God would be manifest everywhere to the inhabitants of that renewed world. Men would act as God would have them act; they would do His will; He would reign in all hearts; that would be the coming of His kingdom. They held fast to this vision, although all round them the world continued to go on its course unmodified: the armies of Rome marched along the roads of the Holy Land; the tax-gatherers demanded money for Cæsar. The iron processes shut them in. Day after day came and went by; but the Day of the Lord did not come.

And then they had met with Jesus.

The significance of Jesus to them was that in Him the wonder-world seemed to be breaking again into this one. There was a mysterious something about His Person which made them ask each other the question, which made other people ask the question, "Who is He?" It is often said that our Fourth Gospel disagrees with the earlier Synoptists, because in it Jesus puts His Person prominently forward in His discourse, makes tremendous Messianic claims, whereas there is little of this in the Synoptists; in those He talks about the Father, rarely about Himself, and then only by slight indications. It may be beyond our power to-day to say how far the discourses of the Fourth Gospel reproduce things actually said by Jesus on earth, but it is to be noted that in the Synoptists, too, the supreme significance of the Person, Jesus, is emphasized in another way. We may be made to feel that something is supremely important in two ways. One way is by having it plainly put before us in discourse. That is the way in which the Fourth Gospel emphasizes the significance of the Person of Jesus. The other way is by making it a mystery, something which it is the crowning spiritual achievement to apprehend. Jesus in the Synoptists says little about His Person, but when He has led His disciples to the ultimate question which is to crown all their intercourse with Him, the question does not relate to any general truth about God or the principles of human conduct; it is the question, Who He is. "Who do men say that I am? Who do you say that I am?" The mystery. I do not think that the truth about His Person is made in this way by the Synoptic Jesus any less important, less central, than it is by the Jesus of the Fourth Gospel.

The men who consorted with Jesus came to feel that a light from the wonder-world somehow surrounded this Man, shone out from what He said, what He did. They declared that they had actually seen things happen which could only be the wonder-world breaking in on this one—a storm at sea suddenly cease when He commanded it, five barley loaves feed five thousand people. Once when they were in their boat on the lake at nightfall, in difficulties because the wind was contrary, He had come to them, they said, walking on the water. They were familiar, too, with certain abnormal states befalling men and women which came, they were sure, not indeed from God's wonder-world, but from a dark world of evil beyond the confines of this one, things of horrible power breaking into the midst of this world, uncanny and terrifying. Sometimes this dark world in the persons of the poor tormented demoniacs came into contact with the wonder-world surrounding Jesus. When it did, the dark world was vanquished, was driven back; the power in Jesus proved itself incalculably greater. The result seemed to foreshadow that final destruction of evil some day by the wonder-world of God.

It was more than foreshadowing; it meant that the expectation of the wonder-world's coming to change the processes of this one, so long yearned for in vain, had actually begun. And Jesus Himself is said to have endorsed this view. "If I by the finger of God cast out devils, then is the kingdom of God come upon you." Already there. "The kingdom of God" —another saying attributed to Him—"is within you." And by that He almost certainly did not mean any system of unchanging spiritual values recognized or realized by man in his inner life—the way in which the saying has been commonly understood in modern times; He meant that the supreme event was so near that already the thrill and tremor of its approach was in the hearts of men.[1]

Then all hopes collapsed when the crucial trial seemed to come between the power embodied in Jesus and the physical forces of this world. If a single man unarmed was pitted against the police of the Temple and a squad of Roman soldiers, the result, according

[1] It is sometimes said that the saying should be translated "among you," not "within you." But it is questionable whether in Greek ἐντὸς ὑμῶν could mean "among you," except where a contrast is emphasized between the limits of a particular group and everything outside it (as in Xenophon, *Hellen.* ii. 3. 19). It would certainly not be the ordinary way of saying "among you" in Greek. On the other hand, our Lord talked Aramaic, not Greek, and there *is* one Aramaic phrase which may mean both "within you" and "among you" (G. Dalman, *Words of Jesus*, p. 145). It is possible that our Lord used that particular phrase, meaning "among you," and that it was wrongly translated into Greek by someone who thought He meant "within you." Thus we cannot say for certain that He did not mean "among you," though it would be easy to express "within you" unambiguously in Aramaic, by a phrase meaning literally "in your hearts." We do not know what Aramaic phrase our Lord used, but if we suppose that the Greek rightly represents what He said, and if we understand the saying in the way suggested above, that appears to me simplest.

to the processes of this world, would be a speedy suppression of the single man. Of course, if there was a wonder-world and the wonder-world could reverse the processes of this one, the power of numbers and weapons might be turned to nought. Now the disciples saw it put to the test. The result was an easy victory for the normal processes of the world, for numbers and weapons. The single man was quickly mastered and put upon the cross. So there had been no real break in the sequence of physical events. It had been all an illusion. You were back again where you were before, only the heart broken by the failure of a soaring hope.

Then, a few days later, events occurred which brought hope back with exultation. The disciples of Jesus discovered that He was not dead, but alive. Many of them had seen Him, had heard Him speak. So, after all, the wonder-world *had* broken into this one. The death to which, according to the processes of this world, everything, good or bad, must succumb in the end, had proved unable to arrest this Man's vital activity. The question is often raised to-day whether this belief in the Resurrection of Jesus necessarily involves a belief in the reanimation of His material body, in the story of the Empty Tomb. Is it not sufficient if the disciples received assurance that Jesus, the individual Person, had passed through bodily death into another life in the unseen world? It is the survival of the Person, not the reanimation of the body, which is important. If this was all, it is hard to see why the experiences in which the disciples believed that they saw and talked with the risen Jesus should have made the enormous difference they did. Most Jews believed that persons continued to exist in the unseen world after bodily death. It might have been comforting to the disciples to have a demonstration of this in the case of their Master, but it would not have taught them anything new, anything distinctive about Jesus. On the other hand, I do not myself think it wise to make the distinctive thing in the Resurrection of Jesus the reanimation of His material body. It seems impossible to square the different accounts given us in the New Testament of the events of those transcendent days; I do not see how we can ever know precisely what occurred. What then was the distinctive thing about the Risen Lord? It was that His Person was continuously active in this world—not only continuously active, but active on a much vaster scale, with a reach and power that Jesus had never had in the limitations of His earthly life. I think this is what is meant by St. Paul in the first verses of his Epistle to the Romans. "According to the flesh," that is, in the life on earth, Jesus had been a man of the seed of David, but by the Resurrection He entered on a new life, acting through a spirit of holiness, diffused in the world of men, a life marked by such power as showed this Person who, as a man, was the Son of David to be in His spiritual activity the Son of God.

The expectation which the disciples of Jesus had had, when He was with them in bodily presence, of a kingdom of God soon to come, which would bring to an end the iron processes of things on earth and interpenetrate this world with the heavenly wonder-world, did not grow any dimmer now that His presence was spiritual, not bodily. It grew stronger, more confident. Because they had seen the iron processes already broken through by His Resurrection. In the case of their Leader, the expected change of things, the wonder-world, had already begun to come. They had direct demonstration of the conquest of death. Perhaps it is hard for us, for whom the Resurrection of Jesus lies nineteen hundred years behind, to realize the thrill and exhilaration which it must have meant for those for whom it was an event quite close, in their own experience, something that happened yesterday, a year or two ago. Someone whom they had personally known, as a Person of their company, they had seen and talked to, alive, after He had died and His body had been buried! After this why should their faith falter at the promise of any wonder? They went all the rest of their lives with the reality of the wonder pressing upon them. And to all the first generation of Christians in the cities of the Roman world, the wonder was still something that had happened in their own time, amid the common processes of the everyday world; they could hear eyewitnesses affirm, " We ourselves have seen."

It is not surprising that with this event already a fact, they should have found it easy to believe that the processes of the existing world would soon be broken off by the overwhelming inrush of God's wonder-world, that Jesus would return upon the clouds and that they themselves and the dead members of their company would rise to meet Him in the air. " Father, thy Kingdom come, thy will be done on earth as it is done in heaven "—the prayer Jesus had taught them—it might happen to-morrow. The stillness of any night might be suddenly shattered by the archangel's trumpet. The events that were happening now in the world around them, the movements of the Roman power, wars, famines, earthquakes, social distress—what could any of it matter so much, when all existing earthly conditions might the next moment be swept away? " But this I say, brethren," Paul wrote to the Corinthians, " the time is short, that henceforth both they that have wives be as though they had none, and they that weep as though they wept not, and they that rejoice as though they rejoiced not, and they that buy as though they possessed not, and they that use this world, as not using it to the full, for the form of this world is passing away."[1] The wonder-world's enormous superiority of power over the processes of this one would be demonstrated for all men to see.

The processes of the world went on. Paul died, as any other man dies, according to natural law, when his head was struck off by the executioner's sword. All the members of the Christian community died in the natural way, by disease or accident or martyrdom. The irruption of the wonder-world did not come. The Church might continue to say that one day the Return of Jesus in glory would really happen, but meanwhile the iron processes which shut men in and doomed everything living sooner or later to death went on undeflected. The next generation died, and the next. It grew to be a hundred years since men had seen, or said they had seen, the risen Jesus. It grew to be two hundred years, to be three hundred, to be ten hundred, nineteen hundred. The laugh seemed on the side of the iron processes; their kingdom had continued unbroken after all. Did you really think, they seemed to say to mankind, that you had found a break, a way of escape? Surely you can see now it was an illusion. Here we are still as dominant as ever. You can nurse all manner of imaginations about a wonder-world on the other side of death; but all you see is that men die, that they die to-day precisely as they died ten thousand years ago.

The expectation with which the infant Church went forth into the world, which gave it buoyancy and courage, has not been realized. That cannot be denied. But in spite of that the Church has gone on;

[1] 1 Corinthians vii. 29, 30.

there are still to-day not a few Christians who seek, as earnestly and strenuously as ever, to make their lives conform to the Spirit of Jesus, to advance His cause in the world. This is itself very wonderful. If the wonder-world has not broken in, as the early Christians expected, it is marvellous that the failure of the great expectation has not proved fatal to the Church. One might have expected that after the Church's challenge to the processes of the world had led apparently to such complete refutation by fact, that would have been the end of it. Somehow it has not. That is very like a miracle. That in the Church of to-day lives of spiritual beauty and power with strong faith in the risen Jesus continue to be presented to men must mean that there is some mysterious source of vitality in this Body which has enabled it to survive even the non-fulfilment of its great hope. The credit of Jesus Himself might seem to have been involved. For there were sayings attributed to Him. "Verily I say unto you, that this generation shall not pass till all these things shall happen."[1] "Verily I say unto you, that there be some of them that stand here, which

[1] Mark xiii. 30. Study of the Bible in the last fifty years has convinced most educated Christians that, while the report of the words of Jesus in our Gospels is substantially true, the record is not exempt from human fallibility in detail. In this case too, God committed His treasure to earthen vessels, as in other operations of His Church. It might have seemed to us more effectual if God had established, for the presentation of the new life in action, men who never sinned, and, for the declaration of doctrine, a book which contained no particle of human infirmity. God saw fit to work otherwise. To those adhering to the older tradition it may mean a loss of comfort, if they cannot believe that every saying attributed to Jesus in the Gospels was uttered by Him in that precise form, just as if it had been reproduced on a gramophone. On the other hand, it may sometimes bring comfort if we may suppose a slight inaccuracy in the record. In the case, for instance, of this saying attributed to Jesus it is harder for those who think that the thirteenth chapter of St. Mark gives us *verbatim* what Jesus said, in the order in which He said it, than if we may suppose some confusion in the report of those who

shall not taste of death, till they have seen the kingdom of God come with power."[1] In the assemblies of the Church these words of the Founder were continually read aloud; they were copied, as the generations went by, from manuscript to manuscript, and the faith of the Church was not staggered by them! Every day there was flung up to the sky the prayer "Thy will be done on earth as it is in heaven," and every day passed with the prayer not granted, till the tale of days has mounted to nearly two thousand years. To-day we seem as far as ever from the will of God being done an earth, as it is in heaven.

Two thousand years, and man is waiting still and yearning!
Go to thy Father back, bright Herald of the day,
And say "No dawn is come, but only night's returning:
Thy promise, Lord, is long, is long upon the way."[2]

---

remembered His words years afterwards or of those who put that report in writing. It seems probable that Jesus did say on some occasion that the present generation would not pass away till all the things He had spoken of had happened. But He may have been referring only to the destruction of the Temple by the Romans which happened in A.D. 70. In Mark xiii the discourse of Jesus is an answer to a question of the disciples which relates specifically to the destruction of the Temple. In the following discourse a great deal of matter relating to the final coming of Jesus in glory is combined with matter relating only to the siege of Jerusalem by the Romans. Sayings of Jesus uttered separately on other occasions seem brought together to make a continuous discourse; some of them are actually attributed to Jesus on other occasions in our Gospels. As it stands in this patchwork, the saying that all these things will happen in the lifetime of the present generation makes it appear that "these things" are the events of the final coming. The saying originally may have referred only to the events connected with the destruction of the Temple. As a matter of fact, if one changed the place of verse 30 in Mark xiii, making it follow verse 23, the difficulty would disappear.

[1] Mark ix. 1.

[2] Deux mille ans sont passés, et l'homme attend encore:
Ah! remonte à ton Père, ange de l'avenir,
Et dis-lui que le soir a remplacé l'aurore,
Et que le don céleste est trop lent à venir.

A. de Lamartine. "Sur l'Image du Christ écrasant le Mal" in the *Harmonies Poètiques et Religieuses.*

And yet by profession the Christian Church has never given up its hope that Jesus really will return at long last, and the sequence of earthly processes come to an end for humanity. As far back as the second century of our era, some people in the Christian community were beginning to say " Where is the promise of His coming? For since the fathers fell asleep, all things continue as they were from the beginning of the creation." (2 Peter iii. 4.) The iron processes! And they got the stock answer, " With the Lord a thousand years are as one day." But, if this is so, a million years with the Lord are as one day, and there is no more reason to suppose that the kingdom of God will come with power and glory when two thousand years have passed than that it will come when twenty thousand or a hundred thousand or a million years have passed. The word " soon " or " near " or " quickly " applied to the Coming, if taken as a measure of time, is then meaningless.

All through the nineteen hundred years there have occurred moments when the expectation of the Lord's coming, as something really imminent, has flamed up again in the Christian Church. And over and over again the moment has gone by, and the hope once more been relegated to an indefinite future far away. In his Dialogues, written some 570 years after the Resurrection, the great Pope Gregory I offers an explanation why there have been recently so many appearances of the spirits of the dead, more frequent, he says, than in any former age, and his explanation is that the wonder-world is now so soon to break into this one that the partition between them has become thin; the denizens of the other world are beginning to come through; it is the last hour of twilight immediately before dawn. And since that was written some 1340 years of troubled earthly history have gone by.

Look on some 540 years from the death of Pope Gregory, and you find the monk Bernard of Cluny sure that now it really is the last hour, that Christ is returning for judgment.

> The world's last hour is come;
> Sins, mounting, reach their sum;
> The time so evil, "Watch" is the command.
> Stern judgment to fulfil
> On all rebellious will,
> The Judge, the Lord Most High, is near at hand.
>
> The Judge, the Lord, is near,
> To make an end severe
> Of ancient wrong, and vindicate the right,
> To give the just their crown,
> Lift up the soul bow'd down,
> And open wide to men the world of light.[1]

In the nineteenth century the belief that the Return of Christ was to be expected within the next few years prevailed in Evangelical circles. It was especially emphasized in the Irvingite community. One evening, I believe, a large number of the community actually assembled in their Cathedral in Gordon Square, convinced that the Return was to occur that very night, and waited in tense expectation till the grey of the morning. Evangelicals, generally speaking, thought it wrong to mark a precise date for the Return; they only fostered the belief, founded on a study of the prophetic parts of the Bible, that it was to be expected now at any moment. We have reached the year 1940, and up to the time of these words being written the world's processes continue unbroken.

[1] Hora novissima, tempora pessima sunt; vigilemus.
Ecce minaciter imminet Arbiter ille supremus:
imminet, imminet, ut mala terminet, aequa coronet,
recta remuneret, anxia liberet, aethera donet.
The opening lines of Bernard's denunciatory poem (not a hymn) entitled the "Rhythm" or "De Contemptu Mundi."

CHAPTER II

TWENTY CENTURIES OF HISTORY

When the Christian Church thought that the earthly order of things was to come to an end in the immediate future, its attitude to the events of the day could not but be one of relative unconcern. Our attitude cannot be that to-day. Here we have, presented to our consideration, this earthly history of nineteen hundred years—processes in which we see no break, and which, for all we know, may go on unchanged for thousands of years to come. The Father in heaven to whom we pray is not, we believe, regardless of things on earth till He intervenes in some far-off divine event, to which the whole creation moves. We believe that He is the Lord of history, that somehow these iron processes work out to results which are subordinate to His purpose and plan for the whole. This is very difficult. For, look as we may at the events of the centuries behind, at the course of the world to-day, we cannot see how they correspond with any divine plan we can imagine. It is not only that we see no irruptions of another world into the natural processes round us, nothing that can be called "miracle," and that we have to recognize how, over and over again in the past, when men have thought they witnessed such an irruption of the "supernatural" it has proved an illusion, but also we do not see how the belief that through the sum total of natural processes God is working out a design of good, fits the facts. We mean by "God" Someone in whom all good finds its complete realization; if we talk of a divine purpose or plan for the course of events on earth, we can only mean that it is somehow adjusted to secure that the values recognized by the spirit of man—moral goodness, beauty, truth, happiness, fellowship—should be brought by the plan into actual existence to the greatest extent possible, and their opposites—moral badness, ugliness, falsehood, misery and discord—done away. Do we see this in the course of these nineteen hundred years? Newman said that when he looked at the world's movement, hoping to see God in it, he experienced the same unpleasant feeling as he would, if he looked into a mirror, expecting to see his face, and saw no face there![1] Of course we see in human history, in the world round, a great deal of value become actual—lives of men full of beautiful goodness, of heroic courage, we see the beauty which the spirit of man discovers in material things and which the genius of the artist makes plain; we see love and intelligence and happiness. And in all this we may recognize a manifestation of God. To that extent our prayer "Thy kingdom come; Thy will be done on earth, as it is done in heaven" is being answered. But only very partially answered. When we look at the earth as a whole, God's will is as far as ever from being done in it, as in heaven. We see good, but a great deal of the opposite as well—

[1] One may compare what an eminent living historian says regarding the aspect which human history as a whole presents to him: "Men wiser and more learned than I have discerned in history a plot, a rhythm, a predetermined pattern. These harmonies are concealed from me. I can see only one emergency following upon another as wave follows upon wave, only one great fact with respect to which, since it is unique, there can be no generalizations, only one safe rule for the historian: that he should recognize in the development of human destinies the play of the contingent and the unforeseen."—H. A. L. Fisher, *A History of Europe*, I, p. vii.

utterly evil characters, ugliness in the works of men, hatred, brutality and misery. It is a world in which good and evil are mixed in such infinite complications and varieties of shade that it seems to be a matter of subjective mood to pronounce whether the good or the evil predominates. When a popular argument, obvious to any dullard, asserts that the existence of evil in the world proves that the world was not made, and is not ruled, by a good God, Christians, of course, maintain that the argument is not cogent. An answer is indicated. God's omnipotence does not mean that He can do what is self-contradictory. The highest moral and spiritual good can only be realized when creatures endowed with freedom of choice choose good by an act of will. But to suppose that the highest good could be realized without the possibility of wrong choices being made would be self-contradictory, and therefore something which God could not bring about. A world in which good and evil are mingled is the only kind of world in which character may be formed by right choices, and the formation of such character is the supreme good for human creatures—or a necessary condition for the supreme good. Thus for the production of the supreme good, there has to be a world in which evil can occur. I do not think that this argument removes all difficulties; no theory can remove all the difficulties which the existence of evil presents to a believer in God, but it may be taken as pointing to a solution.

What, however, I want to urge here is that this argument, even if taken as showing how a world of mixed good and evil is compatible with the goodness of God, does not show how the time-process is the progressive realization of a Divine plan. This world of mixed good and evil, proceeding by a system of unvarying natural laws, might serve a purpose of good, as a training-ground for human spirits successively passing through it, even if no increase of good is traceable in the balance of things on earth. In order to regard a school as a very good school, it is not necessary to show a continuous improvement of its arrangements from one generation of scholars to another, or a continuous advance in the quality of the generations. It is enough if there is progress in the character and attainments of the individual scholars during the three or four years of their passage through the school. The question whether the history of man on the planet is marked by progress, in the condition of things here and the character of successive generations, has been a good deal debated. There has certainly been an increase of knowledge, and with that increase an increase of power in the use of natural processes for human ends. But whether men are better men now than they were a thousand years ago, or will be better men a thousand years hence than they are to-day, is very doubtful. Yet even if this is not so, the world, as it is, may be seen by God to be the best possible "vale of soul-making."

For Christians indeed there has been one moment of human history at which a new factor entered the world, a factor which meant that a kind of good which had not been there before was thenceforth actual in the medley of good and evil. The Resurrection of Jesus and coming of the Holy Spirit meant that a New Life was operative in those united to Christ's mystical Body. But this entrance of a new thing, although it marked an epoch, does not involve a progress in good between one Christian generation and another. The Divine Life is now always there at issue with evil, but each individual who comes into the world and receives for himself that Life "makes his soul" as the member of a Body which embraces all Christian generations together, without any superiority of the latter generation over the earlier. Of course, such a belief implies that the real end of humanity is not any future transient generation on earth, but the complete union of the Body in the wonder-world beyond death.

Yet for nineteen hundred years the course of events on earth has very extensively affected the conditions under which the men of each successive generation have had to make their souls and exhibit in practice the Divine Life. The Church cannot look with an indifferent eye at this history unrolling itself through the centuries, in the midst of which it has to shape its own course. Christians are not now merely passive spectators of history, but active participants in it. In so far as they are that, they can to that extent bring about the doing of God's will on earth after the pattern of heaven. Yet the course of history has largely been determined by things outside any Christian's power to control—by the sequence of the iron processes of nature, by the will of men who take no account of God's will. When some event occurs which, for that time and in that region, imports the increase of some kind of good and diminution of evil—a great religious movement, an establishment of civil freedom, the overthrow of a tyrant, a blooming of literature and art—it is possible, when the event has occurred, to see how it was prepared for, how the way was made clear for it, by material processes, by the actions of men directed to quite other things—the spread of Christianity, for instance, facilitated by the subjugation of the Mediterranean countries by Rome —and it may be said that here at any rate you see the hand of God guiding history. But when you try to see some scheme in history as a whole which makes for a progressive increase of good over evil, it is a much harder matter. In some particular generation there may be a general happy sense that the world has grown much better. Perhaps there was such a sense in the later Victorian days. And then something may occur which makes all such happy forecasts seem foolish. Take, for instance, the matter of cruelty. If there was one thing upon which people congratulated themselves fifty years ago, it was that the world had grown more humane. The efforts of men like Beccaria for the abolition of torture had been ultimately successful. Within the last twenty-two years, we have seen in two great European countries, Russia and Germany, an outbreak of cruelty on a huge scale. A little more than a hundred years ago Europe was shocked by the book of an Italian patriot, Silvio Pellico, giving an account of his experiences in an Austrian prison. If you read the book to-day, what is likely to strike you is how very mild an Austrian prison of those days was, compared with what we have heard of as done in Russia since 1917 and in Germany since 1933.

To-day when we survey the historical process in which we are involved we have Darwin in our minds. It continues the prehistoric process in which progressively higher types of man arose from the gorilla-like creature who was ancestor of the human race. But there is no reason to suppose that in the historical period the human type has been advancing in bodily physique or in mental faculties or in the virtues of character. It has only been advancing in knowledge and a particular kind of power. In scientific inquiries we can register a progress, the later in date being usually (apart from temporary regressions) superior to the earlier: a scientific book sooner or later becomes out of date, and is superseded. But it is not so in other works of the human spirit—in poetry and art. Homer is never superseded; the Elgin marbles are never made out-of-date by any later works of sculpture. Poetry and art show new forms, as the generations follow one another; they extend their operation to new matter and produce new effects. But the later is not necessarily better than the old, it is different; each has its own worth, permanent worth if it is good poetry and good art; the achievements remain side by side, enriching the human heritage by a variety of good things, but their worth does not depend on their being early or late in the series. You cannot trace a progress in the art of poetry from Shakespeare to Milton, from Milton to Pope, from Pope to Keats, from Keats to Tennyson, from Tennyson to T. S. Eliot. And spiritual and moral character is analogous to literature and art, not to science. The saint of one age has a different material to deal with from that dealt with by the saint of another, and shows a different type of goodness accordingly, but one cannot say that the type of a later age is better than the type of an earlier. It is different, that is all. St. John, St. Augustine, St. Francis of Assisi, Luther, Sir Thomas More, George Fox, John Wesley, Cardinal Newman, Charles Gore—one cannot see in such a series an increasing goodness. No doubt the circumstances of a particular age may give the good men who live in it to some extent erroneous ideas of what is right and wrong in practice. St. Dominic, for instance, may really have been a saint, though he encouraged a horrible persecution of heretics: in that way, there may be a rectification in the forms of conduct recognized by the good men of a later age. But it is quite possible for the man whose ideas of right and wrong are more or less erroneous to be superior in many points of spiritual character to the man whose ideas are more correct—in self-devotion to the good which he sees, in energy of well-doing, in love to God.

We cannot then regard this process of nineteen hundred years as one which has been producing higher and higher types of spiritual good. It would be difficult to say that we can see progress in it, as a whole, in any respect except such as depends on the advance of knowledge and power. You can no doubt see progress in particular spans of the process in particular parts of the globe, though the good acquired may not have extended to other parts of the globe and may have been lost in subsequent spans. In what can such progress consist, if it does not mean the production of higher types of goodness? It may consist in a certain type of goodness being extended to a larger number of people; a larger number, for instance, may be brought at a particular time into active membership of the Christian Church, as in the Methodist movement of the eighteenth century. In consequence of an extension of goodness to a larger number of people, the standards of conduct in society generally, in political life, may be raised, as occurred in England at the end of the eighteenth century, partly, Lecky held, in consequence of the Methodist movement. Or again, the organization of a people's life, economic, social, political, may be changed in such a way as to extend a standard of material well-being, in housing, clothing, food, sanitation, to a larger part, if not the whole, of the community, or to extend to larger numbers an education which enables them to develop their intellectual faculties better and enrich their own lives by what they read and see. Or, the barriers which hinder fellowship between men of one nation and another, of one class and another, may be removed, and enmity replaced, for larger numbers, by friendship. In many of these respects we can point to progress made in many countries during recent centuries—progress here and set-backs there; and there is no reason to doubt that the evils which remain might be reduced or done away, supposing those who have power in any part of the world, rulers or people, went the right way about it.

Thus we are bound to look at this world process in which we are engaged not as something about which it is not worth while to feel great concern, because it is going to end so soon, in the way the first disciples of Jesus did, but as a process in which it is worth while doing all we can to increase the good and diminish the evil.

In each generation there is some particular form and array of evil which confronts the human spirits who at that moment make their passage through this world. No efforts of theirs will bring in the kingdom of God for whose coming Christians pray, because the coming of that kingdom would mean that all men everywhere gave themselves to God to do His will, and our power to make the wills even of our near neighbours other than what they are is very small. But something we can probably, each of us, do to reduce the particular evils which constitute the problem of our time, and if many of us are working for this end together, success is the more likely. At the present moment we are confronted with evil in a gigantic form—another war between nations armed with modern scientific means of destruction, a war in which our own nation is a belligerent. But it is not war only; it is the spirit, the temper, the cast of mind behind the Powers opposed to us which gives its dreadfulness to the evil. Our day sees a concentration of power in Russia and Germany to crush, not only belief in God, but the old standards of behaviour between man and man, respect for truth and reason, an attempt to set up the worship of mere strength, such as may seem to colour our day with the lurid light of the ancient Apocalypses.

This is the problem before us.

For some people it is a difficulty for faith that such a thing should be at all. If God, they say, is the Lord of history, how could He direct the process so as to bring about in the years 1939 and 1940 such an agglomeration of evil? This difficulty appears to me to arise from a superficial view of past history and a misunderstanding of the Christian faith. That faith does not involve the belief that the world gets better and better, and that God always prevents the evil will of men from achieving its purpose. There is no greater difficulty in reconciling the war of 1939 and 1940 with God's Providence than there is in reconciling the Diocletian Persecution of the years 303-313. If the late Canon Charles's interpretation of the Book of Revelation is right, the author supposed that the Beast would put every Christian in the world to death, but that did not diminish his belief in the coming establishment of the kingdom of God. Yet there *is* a problem for faith in the world process as a whole and all the evils which emerge in its course. How are we in any sense to conceive of God directing or "overruling" history, if He allows the evil will of men so largely to determine it? And another problem, or perhaps the same one otherwise expressed: To what end is God directing the process? If you saw a steady increase of the proportion of good to evil in the world, as the centuries went by, you could point to that as the reason of God's government. But if you admit that this cannot be seen, to what consummation is the world process tending, what end that will make the whole of it, looked back upon, to have been worth while? What of the Christian hope, the return of the Lord Jesus in power and glory? If that hope was in so far an illusion as the Return was expected in the immediate future, in what sense must Christians to-day hold to the hope, as *not* an illusion? " Surely I come quickly. Amen. Even so, come, Lord Jesus "—the last verse but one of our Bibles—has that ceased to have any meaning at all for the Christians of 1940 *anno Domini*, a year we still reckon as a " year of the Lord "?

CHAPTER III

IRAN AND ISRAEL

AMONG only two peoples a religion has arisen which has attached a high value to history, as a process guided by a Divine purpose to an ultimate kingdom of God, a consummation in which good will triumph and evil be annihilated or vanquished. One of these peoples spoke an Aryan tongue, one a Semitic—the ancient Iranians, the ancient Hebrews. In Iran a new religion was founded by the prophet Zarathushtra, whom Greeks and Latins spoke of as Zoroaster. When he lived and preached is uncertain: the opinion of scholars varies from a date about 1000 B.C. to the middle of the sixth century B.C. A great central desert surrounded by a belt of mountainous country is the land inhabited by the Persians and their Iranian kinsmen; only the fringe of the desert at the foot of the mountains affords green pasture for cattle and a settled habitation for men: in the steppe towards the desert nomad peoples, shifting from one ill-watered region to another, can pick up a living. In the earliest documents of the Zoroastrian scriptures composed, it is thought, by the prophet himself, the Gâthâs, we see a population of industrious farmers, stock-raisers, living always under the menace of raids from the nomads of the steppe, marauders who break in, harry or kill the cattle and destroy the useful works of the settled land. We see also chieftains, heads of clans, who add to the afflictions of the farmers, and follow a primitive form of religion which includes the slaughtering of cattle, and frenzy got from the *haoma* drink in nocturnal orgies. It is to this people of farmers that the prophet Zarathushtra comes with his gospel of encouragement. There is always going on in the world, he tells them, the fight between good and evil, between those who serve the Creator, the "Wise Lord," Ahura Mazda, and those who serve the Spirit of Evil, "the Lie." A dualism runs through all we see: everything, everybody is either on the side of God or on the side of the Evil One. No blurring of the distinction between right and wrong. The work especially pleasing to God is stock-raising and a considerate care for the kine: the ox who is caused to suffer sends up his cry to the throne of God. The servants of the Evil One are, most signally, the marauders of the steppe who hurt the cattle and break up the order of settled life, or the followers of the dark primitive religion. The traditional deities of Iranian polytheism—Mithra, Anahita—the prophet ignores: his religion recognizes virtually but One God, though with God there are associated a number of Powers whose character wavers between that of semi-personified modes of the Divine activity and man's response and that of personal beings, a kind of angels—the Holy Spirit, and the six "Immortal Beneficent Ones," Good Thought, Right, Kingdom, Piety, Welfare, Immortality. But what gave its thrilling force to Zarathushtra's gospel was his announcement that the fight between the servants of God and the servants of the Evil One was coming soon to the great final consummation whereby God would sweep away evil and make a new world in which the righteous would enjoy eternal happiness. The servants of the Evil One would be cast into eternal misery in the "House of the Lie." There would be a great Judgment in which men would be separated for happiness or misery strictly according to their works, and Zarathushtra brought in the old traditional figure of the Bridge—"the Bridge of the Separator," he called it. Not only the righteous living at the Last Day would enter into bliss, but there would be a resurrection of the dead in their bodies. Zarathushtra expected apparently that he would live to see the coming of the kingdom of God, that he would be at the head of his followers, when it came, and that in the separation of the righteous and the wicked he would be appointed by God to act as judge.

We have in the Gâthâs no systematic statement of Zarathushtra's gospel; they are devotional outpourings, as the Psalms are, and presuppose the doctrines of the religion as known. But putting together the incidental allusions they contain to the prophet's eschatological expectation, we seem to get the substance of it as just described. The prophet died, and the kingdom of God had not come. The prophet died, but his religion survived and the Iranians in the fourth century B.C. seem, as a people, to have adopted it. But it had undergone modifications since the prophet had left it to his first followers. For one thing little bits of the older superseded paganism had crept back into it. Mithra and Anahita were worshipped, as subordinate to the "Wise Lord." It had become in other ways elaborated into a hard-and-fast scheme. The dualism had been sharpened: the Wise Lord and the Evil One were regarded as almost on the same level, to start with, two "twin" Powers who came into being together at the beginning of things, though the supremacy of the good Power was so far maintained, that in the great consummation the Wise Lord would utterly vanquish and annihilate the Evil One. Existing things, according to the doctrine now received, had been created, some part of them by God, and some part of them by the Evil One. Cattle, asses, dogs, goats, falcons, crows, hedgehogs, were creations of God; wolves, snakes, frogs, tortoises, locusts, flies were creations of the Evil One; it was a work of piety to show regard for the good animals and to kill the evil animals. The eschatological expectation came to be embodied in a precisely marked-out scheme of successive ages. As the scheme is given in the books belonging to the period after the restoration of the religion in the third century A.D., six thousand years are to elapse from the creation of man to the final consummation when evil is vanquished and the new world of bliss brought in for the righteous after the resurrection. Since a date had then been fixed by tradition for Zarathushtra's birth which corresponds with 630 B.C. in our reckoning, and Zarathushtra is said to have been born thirty years before the end of the third millennium from the creation of man, this would put the creation of man at 3600 B.C., and the great consummation when history ends in the coming of God's Kingdom would come in A.D. 2400. This relegation of the consummation to a distant future made the outlook of a Zoroastrian in the third century of our era very different from that of the first followers of the prophet. Yet both alike looked on human history as a process leading up to God's great final triumph over evil.

How early this scheme of ages was framed we do not know, but we do know that the Zoroastrian Persians had either this scheme or at any rate a scheme resembling it, which divided human history into periods consisting each of a thousand years and which made human history lead to the establishment of a kingdom of bliss, as early as the fourth century B.C. This is proved by a quotation from the Greek historian Theopompus, in which he described the religious beliefs of the Persians.[1] His description does not correspond exactly with the scheme just given, found in the later Zoroastrian books, but this may be either because the Zoroastrians, when Theopompus wrote, had not yet elaborated that scheme, or because Theopompus only gave a loose inaccurate version of what the Persians believed. Greeks in such matters were very sketchy. What we can say for certain is that as early as the fourth century B.C. the Zoroastrian Persians had come to have a scheme of human history of such a type. This is important because it shows Persian eschatology in being, some two hundred years before the rise of apocalyptic literature among the Jews.

One sees the significance of this Zoroastrian view of history—a process in a single line from a unique beginning to a unique end—when one contrasts it with the view of the Indians and the Greeks—a circular recurrence leading nowhere. Indian Monism which held that the manifold universe, the plurality of persons and things, good and evil, was a vain show and that the reality behind it was the One without distinctions, did not lead men to set a high value on events in time or to make life a strenuous fight for good against evil. It was dualism, for which the distinction between good and evil was fundamental and life a real fight, which made this world important and attached eternal issues to the part men played in it. If the work of Zoroastrianism is measured by the proportion of the human race which has definitely adhered to it, its fortunes, as a religion, seem poor. It did not spread beyond the Iranian table land, and when that region was conquered in the seventh century A.D. by the Mohammedans, the Iranians

[1] Quoted by Plutarch, *On Isis and Osiris*, 47 (370 B).

abandoned their ancestral religion for Islam, except one small community which still lingers on at Yezd,[1] and another little body of men who fled to India and founded there the estimable Parsee community. The Zoroastrian religion in its Parsee form might seem rather a desiccated affair of ritual observances, the contrast between it and the religion of Zarathushtra being analogous to the contrast between Rabbinic Judaism and the religion of Isaiah, though the Parsees, a community resembling in some ways the Jews or the Quakers, are characterized by a high reputation for business ability and a generous philanthropy. But if it is true that Judaism in the last two centuries preceding the Christian era was strongly influenced by Zoroastrianism in its eschatological outlook and its view of history, and that the Christian scheme of things in turn was shaped by the Jewish apocalypses, then we must see an extension of Zoroastrianism far beyond the range of its professed adherents; it reaches all over the world wherever there is a branch of the Christian Church. If ideas held by Christians are derived from Zoroastrians, that no more proves them to be untrue than it proves an idea to be untrue, if it is derived from the Old Testament. The Spirit of God may have enlightened Zarathushtra as well as Isaiah.

The other people who regarded history as the unrolling of a Divine plan was the people of Israel. The resemblances between the religion of Zarathushtra and that of the Old Testament prophets are

[1] After this little Zoroastrian community had been regarded for centuries by their Mohammedan Iranian kinsmen as wretched unbelievers, I believe the present Shah has shown them some favour, as representing a relic from the great days of ancient Persia. This is interesting as an instance of a tendency marking our time in other countries—in Turkey, in Germany—nationalism, instead of religion, coming to be the dominant interest.

striking. In both there is the insistence that the One God, the Creator of the world, is characterized by righteous will, that good and evil are a fundamental contrast, that the service of God means strenuous action to reduce the reign of evil in the world and increase that of good, that God will sooner or later intervene to sweep away evil, that in the Day of Judgment the enemies of God will be exterminated and the righteous enter into the kingdom of bliss. With these resemblances there are, of course, differences. Zoroastrianism had a clearer doctrine about the life beyond death for individuals. At death the spirit of the righteous man entered into a world of light and bliss and the spirit of the unrighteous man into a hell of darkness and cold and stench and filthy food. And at the consummation of human history there would be a bodily resurrection, so that all the righteous, at whatever period of history they might have lived, would be united, as a society, in the world of light.

In the religion of the Old Testament prophets, before Daniel (166 B.C.), all that concerns the life of individuals beyond death is vague and dim.[1] When they portray the coming Judgment, which is to crush the wicked and bring salvation to the righteous, they seem to be thinking only of the wicked and the

[1] That this defect in Hebrew religion was sometimes painfully felt may be seen by Psalm lxxxviii, upon which Baethgen comments: "The lack of the hope of a real life beyond death in the Old Testament is to be explained by the strongly developed community-consciousness, in which the value of the individual is lost sight of. The individual has value only as a member of the community and in the forms of the community. The individual feels that, when he is torn out of this fellowship, there is no longer any possibility for him of co-operating in the carrying out of the Divine plan and in the praises of Yahweh, in which Israel's task consists. Thus death appears to him as the absolute negation of all communion with God. Only by degrees does religious experience wrestle its way up from this lower standpoint to one higher and more full of hope." (*Die Psalmen* in Nowack's *Handkommentar zum Alten Testament*, p. 272.)

righteous who will be alive on earth when the Judgment comes. The idea of a resurrection does not appear, except in one passage of Isaiah (xxvi. 19), which is generally believed by scholars to belong to a late insertion in the collection of documents now going under the name of the eighth-century prophet. Ezekiel's vision of the dry bones (Chapter xxxvii) is only a parable of the restoration of the Israelite people, not intended to describe a bodily resurrection of individuals. Of course ideas similar to the Zoroastrian ones regarding the future, including belief in a bodily resurrection, came to be incorporated in Judaism in the century and a half proceeding the Christian era and passed on to the Christian Church, to be an essential part of its creed.

On the other hand, the Hebrew prophets describe much more clearly than the Gâthâs do the kind of conduct in which righteousness consists. We find indeed in the Gâthâs intense moral earnestness, stress laid upon the difference between righteousness and unrighteousness, upon God's care for righteousness, and the contrast hereafter between the lot of the righteous and the lot of the wicked. The changes are rung continually upon names which have a remarkable affinity to the religious phraseology of Jews and Christians—the Holy Spirit and the six Amesha Spentas (" Immortal Beneficent Ones ").

" By his *Holy Spirit* and by *Good Thought*, deed and word, in accordance with *Right*, the Wise Lord with *Kingdom* and *Piety* shall give us *Welfare* and *Immortality*."[1]

But if one asks in what kind of actions righteousness, the conduct pleasing to God, consists, one gets little light upon it, except that a principal part of it is being an industrious stock-breeder, devotedly

[1] Yasna xlvii. 1.

solicitous for the comfort of one's cattle. This may have been, in ancient Iran, an important duty, in so far as the settled orderly life of the farmer was on a higher level of civilization than the life of the nomad marauder, and it was a good work to further the higher type of life. Yet it can hardly be set beside the utterances of the Hebrew prophets in which they tell us what *they* mean by righteousness.

"Establish (just) judgment in the gate." The unrighteous are those that "afflict the just, that take a bribe, and that turn aside the needy in the gate from their right."[1] "Seek judgment, relieve the oppressed, judge the fatherless, plead for the widow."[2] In later Zoroastrian writings the duties of justice and benevolence are clearly inculcated, yet they are mixed up with odd forms of meritorious conduct—killing snakes, tortoises, and the other animals created by the Evil One, and showing extreme regard for the good animals. "It was as grave an offence to refuse food to a dog as to allow a priest to die of starvation."[3] And oddest of all was the doctrine that marriage with the nearest of kin—a man's taking his sister or his daughter to wife—was held to be especially pleasing to God. The Parsees, one must note, have long given up this practice and try to explain away the passages in their sacred books in which it is commended. Of course, one must no more judge of what Zarathushtra's religion was at the outset by what it became centuries later than one must judge of Isaiah's religion by the characteristics of the Talmud.

It is a controverted question how far the apocalyptic expectation, as it grew strong in the Jewish community between the Persian conquest and New Testa-

[1] Amos v. 12, 15. [2] Isaiah i. 17.
[3] A. J. Carnoy in Hastings' *Encyclopedia of Religion and Ethics* art. "Zoroastrianism," vol. xii, p. 865.

ment times, was actually due to the influence of Zoroastrianism. Some critical scholars in recent times have maintained that the Hebrew prophets before the Exile were only denouncers of judgment, and never held out any prospect of restoration. "Zion," Micah said, "shall be plowed as a field, and Jerusalem shall become heaps."[1] The pre-exilic prophets, these critics hold, left it at that. The predictions of a restoration now found in the books ascribed to these prophets are, they say, later insertions. It does not seem possible to demonstrate this view on linguistic grounds, in the case of many of the predictions in question, and other critics hold that some of them were really uttered by the pre-exilic prophets to whom in our Bibles they are ascribed. The question of their date does not matter for our purpose here. The earliest of our written prophecies are those of Amos (about 760 B.C.).[2] Whether the prediction of restoration in Chapter ix. 11-15 was written by Amos or by a later prophet, this at any rate is clear: Amos declared emphatically in the eighth century B.C. that the movements of the peoples in all countries of the earth were directed by the God of Israel. Jehovah was not the God of Israel alone, even though He had chosen Israel to receive a peculiar knowledge of His character and ways. "Are ye not as the children of the Ethiopians unto me, O children of Israel? saith the Lord. Have not I brought up Israel out of the land of Egypt, and the Philistines from Caphtor,[3] and the Syrians from Kir?" (ix. 7.)

We are told by some modern Old Testament

[1] Micah iii. 12.

[2] T. H. Robinson, *A History of Israel*, vol. i, page 370, footnote 1. (Clarendon Press, 1932.)

[3] Caphtor is Crete, the Philistines were representatives of the Minoan civilization, the discovery of whose remains in Crete, Greece and the Ægean has been the great archeological achievement of the last sixty years.

authorities that there are traces of an older, cruder view of their national deity held by the Israelites before the time of Amos, a view which did not differ very much from that which the Moabites held of Chemosh or the Ammonites of Milcom. It may be so. The Israelites may have begun simply with the conviction that Israel was in communication with some invisible supernatural Person, very anthropomorphically conceived, and then they came to perceive that the Some One who was there, the Some One behind the figure of their childish imagination, was the Lord of the whole earth. Might we not then equally say that behind the Moabite conception of Chemosh and the Ammonite conception of Milcom there was the universal God? I think in a sense one must affirm this of all the gods which men have worshipped in earnest. "What therefore ye ignorantly worship this set I forth unto you." The Zeus of the poet Aratus, according to Acts xvii, was the true God whose offspring all men are, faultily conceived.[1] No idea which men have of God is wholly false; no idea is wholly true. In the truest conception which any man has of God there is some distortion, some wrong admixture, to say nothing of the mere imperfection, which comes from the defects—what old writers called in this connexion the imbecility—of all human minds. And between the truest conception and such a conception as the Moabite might have of Chemosh there are indefinite degrees of the proportion of truth to error in different conceptions. Israel is rightly regarded as the people chosen from among all peoples for a special mission because, with however crude a conception of Yahweh or Yaho the Israelites may have started, the Person behind the conception caused it to be changed and corrected and enlarged for them,

[1] Acts xvii. 13-28.

as time went on, till He was known as "the Father of our Lord Jesus Christ"—or, shall we rather say, known as the Father, the Son and the Spirit. Nothing like this happened in the case of Chemosh; very much less happened in the case of Zeus.

To go back to Amos, he had not only come to know Jehovah as the Lord of the whole earth who directed the destinies of other nations, just as much as He did that of Israel, he had come to apprehend a particular characteristic of Jehovah's rule, a characteristic which was the essential thing in the presentation of God by later prophets and by the religion of Judaism. The Power who ruled the world cared supremely for righteousness. And righteousness, Amos and the later prophets insist, includes the behaviour of men to men—justice in judgment, consideration for the weak and poor. According to the principle on which God rules the world, well-doing always procures well-being; the goods which all men value, riches, health, security against enemies, these are attached to righteous conduct; the judgment of God falls sooner or later upon the wicked, bringing them to impoverishment, disease, subjection, premature death. It was not only the behaviour of men in the community of Israel, Amos declared, which Jehovah noted for reward or punishment. Because the Syrians, the Philistines, the Phœnicians, the Edomites, the Ammonites had committed atrocities or had been hard and treacherous in their raids upon the Israelite borders, the palaces of their own kings would be burnt down by enemies and their own people carried into captivity. Similarly, if Israel encountered defeat and subjugation, famine or any other disaster, it was because of the sins committed by the Israelites—the oppression, for instance, of the poor by the rich, or the evil things connected with the idolatrous worship at the local shrines. The earlier prophets think rather of the judgments of God upon the nation, as a whole, upon individuals only so far as they suffer as members of the nation in defeat, massacre, captivity. Writers of later books of the Old Testament—Ezekiel, Proverbs, Ecclesiasticus—insist upon the nexus between well-doing and prosperity in the case of individuals.

> The fear of the Lord prolongeth days:
> But the years of the wicked shall be shortened.
> The righteous is delivered out of trouble,
> And the wicked cometh in his stead.[1]

"I have been young, and now am old," a Psalmist says, "yet never have I seen the righteous forsaken, nor his seed begging their bread."[2]

This firm confidence in the nexus between well-doing and prosperity was as far as possible from being a logical generalization from observed facts. To an unprepossessed consideration the facts of the world showed a multitude of natural processes, following out a uniformity of causes and effects, and largely determining the well-being or ill-being of each individual, while his being righteous or wicked had nothing to do with it.

> Streams will not curb their pride
> The just man not to entomb,
> Nor lightnings go aside
> To give his virtues room;
> Nor is that wind less rough which blows a good man's barge.

Many people could tell the Psalmist that they had seen quite often earthly prosperity depart from a righteous man and his seed begging their bread. The

[1] Proverbs x. 27, xi. 8.
[2] Psalm xxxvii. 25.

Psalmist in his statement imposes in a daring masterful way his conception of what ought to be upon the facts.

The incompatibility of the facts of the world with the traditional doctrine regarding the nexus between well-doing and prosperity is, of course, the theme of the book of Job. The book arrives at no explanation: the ways of God are inscrutable, all man can do is to abase himself with the recognition of his own ignorance and unworthiness. One may note that the difficulty was not peculiar to Israel. Other peoples have conceived their gods as caring in some degree for goodness, and to that extent they too have felt the facts of the world to be a problem.

"Dear Zeus," says the Greek poet Theognis,[1] "I am amazed at you. You rule over all, high in honour and might, and you know well the mind and temper of every man, and your power is the greatest that there is, how is it that you do not hesitate to assign one lot alike to the wicked and the just, whether a man's mind be turned to temperance or to the frowardness of sinners?"

Here is the same problem as that of Job, but because the Hebrews emphasized the righteousness of God with much greater seriousness and consistency than the Greeks did (I except Plato), the problem was more grievous and agonizing for Job than for Theognis.

Now what are we to-day to make of all this? "Prosperity," said Bacon, "is the blessing of the Old Testament, Adversity of the New." And perhaps there are people who think that God's way of dealing with men really did differ B.C. from the way He has dealt with them A.D. If the Psalmist stated that God never let the seed of a righteous man beg their bread, that

[1] Lines 373 ff.

was true, they suppose, when he said it; but since the beginning of the Christian era, God has quite commonly permitted righteous men to die in adversity and their seed to beg their bread. The book of Job shows that the Christian era made no such difference in this respect to the facts of the world; it was the sore problem then that prosperity and adversity did not correspond in man's experience with goodness and wickedness. The assertion that the good were bound to prosper was just as much the forcing of a prepossession upon the facts then in Old Testament times as it would be now.

CHAPTER IV

WELL-DOING AND WELL-BEING

THE truth is that man all over the world has felt that there ought to be a nexus between well-doing and well-being. But in Israel this feeling had peculiar intensity, as the conviction expressed with such passionate emphasis by the prophets spread, that Jehovah's great characteristic was His caring supremely for righteousness and that Jehovah was ruler of the world. Men did not gather belief in the nexus between well-doing and well-being as a generalization from the facts of the world; they brought the belief, as a deliverance of the human spirit, to their consideration of the facts of the world. The facts of the world do not confirm the belief. This difficulty has been met by men in four ways.

The way of the Hebrew prophets and writers of Proverbs was, as we have just seen, to force their conviction upon the facts. They shut their eyes to all the cases in which goodness and prosperity, wickedness and adversity, failed to go together, and noted only cases in which they did, as a manifestation of God's righteous judgment. The good man might, they saw, temporarily fall into adversity, but he was sure to be brought out of it by God and restored to happiness. The wicked man might prosper for a time, but he was sure in the end to come to grief. Suppose the good man's adversity continued without any deliverance coming, it could be explained by saying that he was not really as good as he seemed to be; he was being punished for some hidden sin, invisible to the eyes of men. That was the theory put to Job by his friends. The Psalmist who was troubled by seeing the wicked in prosperity, who in some of his utterances touched the height of Old Testament religion —" Whom have I in heaven but Thee? And there is none upon earth that I desire beside Thee"—the same Psalmist still looked for a solution of his problem in his assurance that the wicked would sooner or later fall from their temporary prosperity into misery.

> Surely thou settest them in slippery places:
> Thou castest them down to ruin.
> How are they become a desolation in a moment!
> They are utterly consumed with terrors.[1]

One may see a modernized form of the Old Testament conviction in Professor John Macmurray's formula, that evil, without any added punishment, is essentially self-destructive. The phrase is one of very

[1] Psalm lxxiii, 18, 19. It might be thought that the Psalmist is thinking of pains in the other world beyond death, because in verse 4 he says of the wicked (in our translations) " there are no bands in their death," implying that their prosperity continues up to the end of earthly life. But the Hebrew characters rendered " in their death " are almost certainly wrongly pointed, and the verse should be translated

> " For they have no bands [or troubles],
> And their body [or " their strength ": the Hebrew word is used nowhere else and its meaning can be only guessed at] is sound and firm."

Thus it is probable that when the Psalmist speaks of the wicked being cast down into ruin, he means that they will come to a crash sooner or later in this life. If in verse 24 " and afterward receive me to glory " is rightly translated we have the Psalmist's own hope of glory in the life beyond, but the Hebrew text is odd (literally " and take me after glory ") and probably corrupt. According to an emendation of Wellhausen's what the Psalmist wrote would be rendered " and drawest me after thee by the hand." But Wellhausen himself came to be dissatisfied with this conjecture.

indefinite meaning, and I find it impossible to get much sense out of it, if one's view is limited to the horizon of earthly things. Does it mean that an evil, an unjust, state of things, brought about by acts of human will, is essentially impermanent? If so, the statement is true, but not of great significance, because every earthly state of things is essentially impermanent. A just state of things, no doubt, has a better chance than an unjust one of enduring, because the unjust state will keep alive in the minds of a great many people the desire to change it. It is true to say in that way that the unjust state of things carries in itself the causes of its dissolution. Yet some unjust states of things have endured for hundreds of years, and some relatively just states of things have been brought to a speedy end by accidents of the environment. Or does it mean that the individuals who will evil are sooner or later destroyed by the evil they have willed? Sometimes, no doubt, they are, but very often their earthly lives are not sensibly shortened by it. I cannot help here being reminded how my aunt, Mrs. Mortimer, the authoress of *Peep of Day* and *Reading Without Tears*, used—so I have been told—to hold up, as a warning to the younger generation, an old gentleman belonging to our family, whose death—at an age well over eighty—was brought on, she insisted, by the excesses of his youth. Or does it mean that anyone who wills evil finds the result in the end disappointing and bitter, finds that, while he chose the evil *sub specie boni*, because of the good he believed he saw in it, he has in truth missed his true good by choosing it? It is a cardinal doctrine of Christianity that this is so. But Christianity only affirms that it is so, because it extends its view of the individual's existence beyond earthly life. Anyone who has chosen evil in this life, will have, after bodily death, that experience, whatever it may be, described symbolically as "standing before the judgment seat of Christ," and then the evil quality of his earthly life will be revealed to him, and he will endure the pain of seeing the good which he has lost. If the view is limited to earthly horizons it would be impossible to show that disappointment and bitterness always follow the choice of evil. No one, of course, is perfectly satisfied under earthly conditions, yet many people whose lives are selfish throughout, but moderately and judiciously selfish, seem to enjoy a higher measure of content, than many people of the most devoted goodness, who suffer perhaps from a naturally fretful temperament or from dyspepsia. Selfish or sensual men of a hale bodily habit may, when they draw near the end of a long life, feel that they have had, on the whole, a good innings and as much enjoyment as should satisfy a reasonable man. It is hard to see how we could pronounce that evil, within the compass of such a life, has proved self-destructive. Or is it meant that, though such selfish persons are content with what they have got, someone who looked at their lives from a higher point of view, would see that there was a much greater good which they might have had, and which they have missed because of their selfishness? That cannot matter to them much if they continue, up to the moment when their existence is finally and utterly terminated by death, ignorant of their loss and without regrets.

In fact, I think that we may say about this theory, of the self-destructiveness of evil within the compass of earthly life, just what was said about the Old Testament belief that the righteous was sure to prosper. There is behind it a true conviction that evil ought to be self-destructive, and is ultimately self-destructive if the universe is rightly ordered.

But it tries to see this conviction verified within too narrow a compass, and so forces its theory upon the facts of life in the teeth of experience. Thus it becomes a falsehood similar to that of Job's friends, which had to the men of that day a sound of piety, just as this theory has to some people to-day a sound of profundity, but is, I fear, meaningless for all that.

A second way in which men have met the difficulty is by asserting that well-doing and well-being, in spite of what appears to the contrary, always *are* joined together, because to have a good will is happiness in itself and it does not require any accession of pleasant circumstances. Even if every conceivable adversity befalls the good man it is sufficient for him that he is good. Similarly, one need not be troubled even if the wicked go on prospering up to the end, because all the time they have sufficient punishment in the mere fact that they are wicked. No further punishment is required. This way of reconciling man's fundamental conviction with the facts of the world is the way of the ancient Stoics and of some high-brow people in modern times.

It can only, I think, be by maintaining a strained unnatural attitude of mind, out of a kind of priggish self-satisfaction in feeling themselves superior to the multitude, that people can find this explanation of things adequate. A man's happiness does, if complete, involve the absence of pain and the satisfaction of those desires which belong to the human spirit—the desire for knowledge, the desire for beauty, the desire to exercise capacities in effective action, the desire for communion with other persons in interest and love. A man for whom all such desires were frustrated and who was in continuous pain could not be said to enjoy well-being, however good he was, except by someone who wants to maintain a paradox which he knows in his heart to be absurd. The fundamental conviction that well-doing and well-being ought to go together cannot be satisfied unless the well-being is something beside the well-doing, and consists in an absence of pain and a satisfaction of desire.

The third way in which the difficulty has been met is by the belief in reincarnation, general in Hindu India. According to this, the amount of well-being is adjusted by the law of Karma to the amount of well-doing with minute exactness, only the adjustment does not take place within the compass of a single life upon earth, but in the series of lives upon earth which the same person goes through. The beauty of this theory is that it enables you to look at the facts without blenching. The most monstrous case of a good man visited with continuous adversity need not trouble you, because you can always say that he is reaping the consequences of his wrong-doing in a former life, and that he will enjoy the fruit of his present well-doing in the next life. I do not propose in this connexion to go into the objections which may be raised to the doctrine of reincarnation and Karma. Those objections, which are grave from a Christian standpoint, may be found stated in a recent book by Sydney Cave,[1] and anybody who wants to confute them should deal with Dr. Cave, who knows more about Indian religion than most of the people who talk about it.

There is a fourth way of meeting the difficulty. It agrees with the doctrine of reincarnation in believing that the life each man is now living on earth is a very

[1] *Hinduism or Christianity?* by Sydney Cave, Principal, New College, London; Professor of Theology in London University. (Hodder & Stoughton, 1939.)

small part of his total existence. But it disagrees with the doctrine of reincarnation in holding that the continuation of a man's present life is not a future series of lives upon earth, but an existence in a wholly different sphere of being from the earthly one, in a world inaccessible to our bodily senses. The generations who pass through this world are journeying into that one.

When each individual's total existence is considered, not only the little part of it constituted by his life on earth, it will be seen that the nexus between well-doing and well-being demanded by the human spirit is fully actualized. The good man in this life may suffer adversity the whole time, but the nexus is maintained because all that suffering forms his personality in such a way as to increase his capacities for joy in the life beyond. Similarly the Psalmist was right when he said that the prosperous wicked were set in slippery places and would suddenly be cast down to ruin, because even if a man remains in this life buoyant and jaunty in his wickedness to his last hour, an evil will bears its bitter fruit in the life beyond.

This belief, in some form or other, is widely spread over the world and enters into most of the religions of men. It was strongly emphasized, as we have seen, in Zoroastrianism. It is sometimes combined with the belief in reincarnation, as by the ancient Pythagoreans and Plato and some forms of Indian religion. The good are then conceived to have a pleasurable existence and the wicked an existence of penal torment in the unseen world in the intervals between their successive incarnations in this world. In the religion of the Hebrews, up to the middle of the second century B.C., the belief in a life beyond the earthly one was strangely in abeyance. And just because, at the same time, the nexus between well-doing and well-being was insisted upon by the Hebrews with quite peculiar earnestness, the abeyance of the belief in a future life caused the facts of the world to be for some Hebrews the agonizing problem which they were for the writer of Job and the writer of Psalm lxxiii. When the belief in a future life is there, the problem which the book of Job leaves as hopelessly insoluble for man loses its gravity. The facts of life can then be looked at, as they really are, and no violence need be done them in order to reconcile them with the demand of the human spirit. In the last two centuries before Christ the belief in a future life, in which the demand would be satisfied, became general among the Jews. When Jesus was on earth only the Sadducees, the party of the Jerusalem chief-priesthood, finding that for them this life had many good things, saw no ground for adopting belief in another one. Jesus Himself seems to have taken the belief for granted in those to whom He spoke. He gave it, in His own teaching, outstanding importance.

To show how the lack of correspondence between goodness and prosperity in this world is rectified by the lot of men beyond death is the point of the parable of the Rich Man and Lazarus. " Son, remember that thou in thy lifetime receivedst thy good things, and likewise Lazarus evil things: but now he is comforted, and thou art tormented."[1] Perhaps someone may say that this is a parable attributed to Jesus in St. Luke's Gospel only, and may not really have been uttered by Jesus. Well, if you confine yourself to those sayings of Jesus which are given by St. Mark and one of the other Synoptists, or by St. Matthew and St. Luke together, without Mark, you have sayings enough which make the life beyond death the

[1] Luke xvi. 25.

thing of paramount importance for every individual person. "Blessed are ye when men shall revile you, and persecute you . . . Rejoice and be exceeding glad: for great is your reward in heaven."[1] "If thine eye cause thee to stumble, pluck it out: it is better for thee to enter into the kingdom of God with one eye, than having two eyes to be cast into hell, into the unquenchable fire, where their worm dieth not, and the fire is not quenched."[2] "Lay not up for yourselves treasures upon earth, where moth and rust doth corrupt, and where thieves break through and steal: but lay up for yourselves treasures in heaven."[3] "Many will say unto me in that day (the day beyond bodily death), Lord, Lord, have we not prophesied in thy name? and in thy name have cast out devils? and in thy name done many wonderful works? And then will I profess unto them, I never knew you: depart

[1] Matthew v. 12: Luke vi. 23.

[2] Mark ix. 47: Matthew v. 29; xviii. 9. The phrase about the worm and the fire is a quotation from the end of our book of Isaiah (lxvi. 24) where it is said that the corpses of the rebels against God, who have been killed at the setting up of God's kingdom on earth, will be always on view somewhere near Jerusalem—according to a late Rabbinic authority, the Valley of Hinnom is meant—miraculously preserved, we are probably intended to understand, from being destroyed by the fire and worms that feed upon them. "And they shall go forth, and look upon the carcases of the men that have transgressed against me: for their worm shall not die, neither shall their fire be quenched." Bernhard Duhm concludes his great commentary on Isaiah with the sentence: "It is sad that a book which contains the most glorious, the most sublime, the most significant, the most deeply religious things in the whole Old Testament should end on such a grisly discord." The phrase may of course have been added to the saying of Jesus by St. Mark or his source, because it was associated with the Valley of Hinnom, whose name had been adopted as that of Hell (*Ge-Henna*), in that familiar passage of the Old Testament. The phrase is not attached to the saying of Jesus in St. Matthew. In any case, the saying of Jesus about a man's being cast into Gehenna has as strong documentary support as any saying attributed to Him.

[3] Matthew vi. 19, 20: Luke xvii. 33, 34.

from me, ye that work iniquity."[1] "Many shall come from the east and the west and shall sit down with Abraham and Isaac and Jacob in the kingdom of heaven. But the children of the kingdom (those of the people of Israel who have rejected their king) shall be cast into outer darkness: there shall be weeping and gnashing of teeth."[2] "Fear not them which kill the body, but are not able to kill the soul, but rather fear Him who is able to destroy both soul and body in hell."[3] "Whosoever speaketh against the Holy Ghost, it shall not be forgiven him, neither in this world, neither in the world to come."[4] "Whosoever shall be ashamed of me and of my words in this adulterous and sinful generation; of him also shall the Son of man be ashamed, when he cometh in the glory of his Father with the holy angels."[5] "There is no man who hath left house or brethren or sisters or father or mother or children or lands for my sake and the gospel's, but he shall receive a hundredfold now in this time . . . and in the world to come eternal life."[6]

It is true that the life beyond death was thought of by the Jews rather as a bodily resurrection at the great future consummation of human history than as a continuance of the person immediately after death in another state of being. Yet just as the belief in reincarnation can be combined with belief in a happy or unhappy existence of the discarnate spirit between the incarnations, so, with the Jews, a belief in the future resurrection and a distribu-

[1] Matthew vii. 22, 33; Luke xiii. 26, 27.
[2] Matthew viii. 11, 12; Luke xiii. 28-30.
[3] Matthew x. 28; Luke xii. 4, 5.
[4] Matthew xii. 32; Mark iii. 29.
[5] Mark viii. 38; Luke ix. 26: Compare Matthew x. 33; Luke xii. 8, 9.
[6] Mark x. 29, 30; Matthew xix. 29; Luke xviii. 29, 30.

tion of rewards and punishments, following it at the great Day of Judgment, was combined with a belief that the discarnate spirit also received reward or punishment immediately after death. This appears in the parable of the Rich Man and Lazarus.[1] In the answer given by Jesus to the Sadducees it is the future life after the Resurrection rather than the condition of the discarnate spirit which is in question. For our purposes the difference is not important. What is important is that Jesus, against the Sadducean view, strongly asserts that a person's existence does not end with bodily death but has a continuation in a wonder-world beyond. "Do ye not therefore err, because ye know not the scriptures, neither the (wonder-working) power of God? For when they shall rise again from the dead, they neither marry, nor are given in marriage; but are as the angels which are in heaven." Abraham, Isaac and Jacob in the interval before the Resurrection are still living somewhere, because God calls Himself their God, and "He is not the God of dead men, but the God of the living."[2]

To many people it has seemed something unworthy, this putting forward the idea of reward for well-doing in a future life. How much nobler, they say, when a man dismisses from his mind any thought of reward, when he does what is right because it is right! How much better the Stoic view that virtue

[1] This double judgment, upon the discarnate soul immediately after death and upon the re-embodied person at the Day of Judgment, was, of course, taken over by the Christian Church, and is to-day the established teaching of Catholicism. The problem raised by it—what difference the Resurrection and Day of Judgment then makes—is discussed by Dante. The sufferings of the damned, he says, will be increased, and the joy of the redeemed made more intense, after they have their bodies again at the Resurrection. *Inferno* vi. 103-11; x. 8-112: *Paradiso* xiv. 43-5.

[2] Mark xii. 24-7; Matthew xxii. 29-32; Luke xx. 34-8.

is its own reward and vice its own punishment! This criticism, I think, confuses two quite distinct things. A man ought not to do right for the sake of any reward; he ought to do right, even if his own well-doing were not otherwise ever to be increased at all by his doing right. This is quite true; but the question is whether when we look at the universe, apart from consideration of our own motives for action, we could be satisfied with it, supposing we were convinced that it did not offer any conjunction of well-doing with happiness and wrong-doing with unhappiness. If God is regarded as the Maker and Ruler of the world such as it is, it is His justice which is in question, not our motives. It is the intense conviction that God *is* just which has led men, all the world over, to declare that, somehow or other, the man who does right will ultimately reap happiness and the man who does wrong unhappiness. When Isaiah declared this with prophetic passion, it would be absurd to suppose that he was thinking, all the time, how much he himself was going to get. And it is noteworthy that the two great philosophers who have most strongly insisted upon the disinterestedness of virtue, Plato and Kant, have also found that they could not make sense of the universe unless there were a life beyond death in which happiness was attached to well-doing and unhappiness to evil-doing. An utterance in a dialogue of Plato's is the text regularly cited by those who lay down that the punishment of a vicious man is his being vicious. Yet Plato who makes his Athenian Stranger affirm this,[1] also gives us the myths of the

[1] "In fact, none of us, or few, reckon with the sorest judgment—as the phrase is—on evil-doing, which judgment is that a man grows like those who already are evil, and, as the likeness grows, avoids good men and good converse, and cuts himself off from them, but follows after the other sort and cleaves to them in intimate fellowship, and he who clings to such men cannot but

other world in the *Republic*, the *Gorgias*, the *Phaedo*, expressing his conviction that a man fared well or ill beyond death according to the life he had lived here. It was Kant who insisted that the thing supremely good was a good will, and that obedience to the "categorical imperative" must be in no degree contaminated by any desire for pleasure. Yet Kant also insisted upon the necessity of believing in human immortality because, if the universe was just, happiness must in the end be proportionate to goodness. That was a fundamental postulate of the spirit of man.

Jesus did not stop at affirming that a good man was rewarded by happiness in the life beyond death; he encouraged His disciples to look forward with exultation to the reward: "Rejoice and be exceeding glad, for great is your reward in heaven." And the same thing is found with the representatives of Christianity in later times, not only with those who are commonly thought unattractive, but with those whose charm has won the heart of mankind. Take St. Francis of Assisi. A specimen of his preaching is given us in the *Fioretti* (Capitolo xvii).

"My sons, we have promised great things, but things very much greater have been promised by God unto us, if we observe those things which we have promised, and look forward with assurance to those things which have been promised unto us. Short is the pleasure of the world; but the pains which follow it are everlasting; small is the pain of this life, but the joy of the other life is infinite."

We must admit that anyone who bids men look

do and have done to him what men of that sort naturally do and say. This state then is not *judgment*—for judgment is, like justice, a good—but vengeance, the painful consequence of iniquity."—*Laws* 728. (A. E. Taylor's translation, Dent & Sons, 1934.)

forward to the future reward induces a mode of thinking which has its dangers. The partition between feeling joy in the assurance of what God will give and acting in order to secure the reward is apt to wear thin, and men may slip too easily from one to the other. Mr. Claude Montefiore, while he was concerned to show the spiritual value of a great deal in Rabbinic religion, expressed, with that fine candour so characteristic of him, his judgment that Rabbinic literature does dwell too much upon the exactly measured reward for righteousness, what he called the doctrine of " tit for tat."[1] Whether it is in any sense compatible with the highest goodness to look forward to a reward depends surely on the way in which the reward is conceived. Plato, who found it necessary to believe in a recompense for righteousness and for wickedness in the life beyond, makes a speaker in his *Republic* refer with contempt to the kind of blessed immortality promised by some Orphic religionists who suppose " that the noblest reward for virtue is an everlasting booze! "[2] Christians commonly repudiate the Mohammedan idea of Paradise. But if a man who has seen the greatest good on earth to be the fellowship of human spirits and has lived his life here in accordance with the supreme law of Love looks forward to a state of being in which love will be freed from the restrictions and interruptions of earthly life and have inconceivable scope, is there anything unworthy in the joy of such anticipation? " Amabo nunquam satis," was, we are told, one of the last utterances of that Abbé Huvelin whom Baron Friedrich von Hügel always spoke of as having helped him more than any other man to lay hold of God.

When, with the Christian hope, we turn to the old

[1] *Rabbinic Literature and Gospel Teachings*, 1930, p. 145.
[2] *Republic* ii. 363 d.

Hebrew prophets and writers of proverbs, we may recognize that, while insisting as they did upon the conjunction of happiness with well-doing they were doing violence to the facts of this world, the fundamental conviction which caused them to do so was true, that the conviction was made strong in them by the spirit of God, and that their utterances may in that way be truly called "inspired." They insisted upon this conjunction both in the case of individuals and in the case of nations. The writers of the historical books tell their story so as to show that when Israel sinned the people were overtaken by adversity, captivity under foreign enemies, and so on, and, contrariwise, the prophets declare that if trouble has fallen upon the people, it is because of some national sin. Christians to-day, as has been said, no longer expect to see the correspondence of well-doing and prosperity in this life and are not troubled by the problem of Job. We recognize that, in the case of individuals, the natural processes of the world go forward without any favour shown to goodness rather than to wickedness, and if we forecast the probability or improbability of anyone of our acquaintance being successful in a commercial speculation or enjoying good health during the next ten years, we do not say, "He is sure to succeed," or "He is sure to enjoy robust health, because he is such an exceedingly good man." We consider the circumstances of the market or the report of a doctor on his heart and lungs.

But now notice something odd. Christians have given up expecting to see the correspondence of well-doing and prosperity in the case of individuals, but they still largely keep to the Old Testament view in the case of nations. This is partly due no doubt in England to the extent to which the Old Testament was applied in Puritanism and Evangelicalism to the contemporary world. Just as when Israel did evil in the sight of the Lord it was delivered into the hand of Midian for seven years, or into the hand of the Philistines for forty years, so, if England sinned, the Divine judgment was likely to fall upon it in some kind of adversity. I knew of a widely respected Evangelical clergyman in the early months of the last war who publicly declared his belief that one reason why our armies were less successful than had been hoped in driving the Germans out of France and Belgium was that *The Times* had desecrated the Lord's Day by bringing out a Sunday edition. A maxim to which to-day a very large number of people instantly assent, as a certain truth, is the Old Testament one that "righteousness exalteth a nation"[1]—not in the sense that a righteous nation is on a higher spiritual level, for in that sense the statement would be almost tautological and hardly worth making, but in the sense that a righteous nation enjoys a greater measure of earthly well-being than an unrighteous one. Nor is it only people of distinctly Christian outlook who affirm this. Carlyle and the Victorians who followed him made it one of the things they preached with the greatest fervour that, because the world really was ruled by a righteous Power, national ill-doing was sure to be visited by national distress. The German line, *Das Weltgeschichte is das Weltgericht* (World history is world judgment), is current among many people who make no profession of Christian belief in the sense that the success of a nation in overcoming its rivals and gaining material welfare is the index of greater moral or spiritual worth. How many people say that in the present war we can be confident of victory because our cause is the better one! How many people, if the worser side should win, would

[1] Proverbs xiv. 34.

have their faith in God shaken! In truth, our cause being morally the better one by no means ensures our victory. To say this is no more impious than Job's contention that, in the case of the individual, his righteousness did not secure earthly prosperity. Why should men be ready enough to grant that as true of persons, but shrink from granting it as true of nations? It is no more incredible that a just God should allow a righteous nation to come to grief than that a just God should allow a righteous man to come to grief.

What conceals the falsehood of the statement that a nation prospers according to its righteousness is that certain kinds of wrong-doing do, by natural law, bring suffering and degradation in their train, and certain kinds of virtue do procure a strength which may be used for aggrandizement. A nation in which social injustice reaches an aggravated degree is likely to be vexed by unrest and intestine fighting which will create wide misery at home and weakness in relation to external enemies. A nation in which habits of order, self-discipline, industry, are highly developed will be more likely to prosper in commerce and in war than a slovenly self-indulgent nation. Mr. Aldous Huxley in his *Ends and Means* refers to Dr. J. D. Unwin's book *Sex and Culture* as having shown that a nation in which chastity and self-control in sexual matters is widely observed will be a strong and mentally productive nation.[1] All this is true; but the same things are true in regard to the conduct of in-

[1] "The cultural condition of a society rises in exact proportion as it imposes pre-nuptial and post-nuptial restraints upon sexual opportunity." (*Ends and Means*, pp. 311, 312.)

"'The group within the society which suffers the greatest continence displays the greatest energy and dominates the society.' The dominating group determines the behaviour of the society as a whole." (p. 312.)

"Chastity is one of the major virtues inasmuch as, without

dividuals. A man of regular industrious habits and self-control will be free from the particular kind of pains and discomforts which wait in the end upon idleness and profligacy. In the sense that dishonesty in business may quite probably lead in the end to loss of custom, honesty is the best policy. Yet the man of regular industrious habits who prospers in business may be a worse man, may have a harder, more selfish heart than the profligate wastrel. Righteousness, on the other hand, may issue in a man's being so devoted to the service of his fellow-men or some great cause that he sacrifices his health and his substance in that service. If you are going to lay down what is most likely to secure a man's health and wealth in this life, the cynical advice of the Preacher probably points the way: "Be not righteous overmuch . . . be not overmuch wicked."[1] In the case of a nation, righteousness might lead to its being faithful to its engagements when such fidelity brought upon it great sufferings, which a less righteous nation would have escaped.

While I am writing this chapter, I have been listening on the wireless to a sermon preached on Armistice Day. The preacher insisted with great impressiveness and conviction upon the course of history being ultimately determined by good spiritual forces. Little by little, they would prevail over the opposing forces and make the world better. It seems to me that you have here someone who still affirms in regard to the world at large what Job challenged when it was

chastity, societies lack energy and individuals are condemned to perpetual unawareness, attachment and animality. In another sense, however, chastity can only rank as a minor virtue; for, along with such other minor virtues as courage, providence, temperance, and the like, it can be used solely as a means for increasing the efficiency of evil-doing." (pp. 315, 316.)

[1] Ecclesiastes vii. 16, 17.

affirmed in regard to individuals. It is, of course, true that, if any society of men—a nation, a group—exhibits a prevalence of the goodwill amongst its members, a general spirit of justice and fellowship, this will have been brought about by good spiritual forces, not by any merely material means. If a state of mankind in which such a spirit of justice and fellowship prevails, is ever to come about by any gradual process, that process will be all through the operation of spiritual forces. But I do not think there is any ground for affirming that a nation or a group will come out on the top in the struggle with other nations or groups because the goodwill is more prevalent within it than it is in them. Nor any ground for assurance that the evil will in the world generally is going in any particular reach of time to be subdued by the good spiritual forces operative in this or any other group. Free will means that the evil will may prevail in the world generally, in human history taken in its long reaches, just as it may in individuals, in spite of the good spiritual forces which come to bear upon them.

A report on the facts of the world, just as they are, without any prepossession as to what ought to be, would register that fortunes of individuals and of nations are determined partly by their voluntary actions, partly by processes in the natural world outside their control. So far as their fortunes are determined by their voluntary actions, certain virtues are likely to obviate certain kinds of evil, and to that extent righteousness may be profitable. So far as their fortunes are determined by natural processes, these appear to continue according to uniform physical laws without any relation to human goodness or human wickedness. This is incompatible with the view that God's rule of history means that national wrong-doing always issues in national suffering and humiliation and national right-doing in prosperity. And just as Job challenged the correspondence of right-doing and prosperity in the case of individuals, so the Jews from the second century B.C. came to realize that the correspondence could not be seen with regard to nations in the stretch of human history open to their observation. The solution of the problem was found in the case of human history as a whole on the same lines as it was found in the case of individuals—the correspondence demanded by the human spirit, by faith in God, would be established in the unseen future. The place of the old prophets is taken by the writers of apocalypses.

What distinguishes the writers of apocalypses is that they focus their attention more upon the course of human history, as a sequence of periods, which will end some day in a great consummation when God will crush evil and bring in a state of righteousness, glory and joy. Their view is far removed from that of the Armistice Day preacher, inasmuch as they see no gradual conquest of evil by spiritual forces during the successive periods. The evil will all through retains its power to afflict and oppress the righteous. The greatest triumph of evil is expected precisely at the end of the periods, immediately before its catastrophic overthrow by God. This was very like the Zoroastrian scheme, and quite probably, as has been said, the writers of Jewish apocalypses were influenced by Persian Zoroastrianism. The old prophetic view, written down before there can be any question of Persian influence, showed an affinity to the Zoroastrian view, and this would make the Jews more easily receive suggestions later on from that quarter. If the old prophets did not mark out a sequence of periods as the scheme of human history, the earliest of them, Amos, did, as we have seen, declare that the movements of nations were directed by God. They did not, as the Zoroastrians and Jewish apocalyptists did, speak of a coming world consummation in which the good men of past ages would rise again and all live together in a state of perfected blessedness in the glory of God. But if Amos wrote the conclusion of the book which goes by his name, he did look forward to a restoration of the land of Israel under kings of the house of David, in which the fertility of the soil would be marvellously increased, and the Israelites carried captive in other lands would be gathered as in their national home. And if Isaiah wrote Chapter xi of the book which goes by his name he did anticipate that under the future Davidic king the earth would be to some extent transformed and become a wonder-world, the lion eating straw like the ox, the serpents harmless, and the knowledge of Jehovah universal. We have seen that many modern critics suppose that these passages were attached by later writers to the original prophecies of Amos and Isaiah—though with no very sure proof of their theory. In any case the first chapter of Isaiah, which no one assigns to any other author than the eighth-century prophet, declares that a time is coming when, by God's power, the nation will be purged of its sinners and made a people of ideal righteousness. No doubt he may have thought of the nation, so transformed, as living still, under ordinary physical conditions, in Palestine, and his expectation would thus not have the reach of the later apocalypses; but it was a hope which might easily expand into that view, when once the suggestion came from the Zoroastrian scheme. Hebrew religion and Zoroastrianism both independently believed that history was being guided by God.

There is one great difference in believing that the lack of correspondence between well-doing and well-being in the life of nations, as seen at present, is righted by a future condition of all mankind and in believing that the goodwill of an individual, if matched with unhappiness in this life, will be matched with happiness in the life beyond. In the case of the individual there is real personal continuity between this life and the life beyond, but it is only by a figure of speech that a nation is represented as a single personal agent and the future generations as identical with the generation of to-day. What we call the well-doing or ill-doing of a nation is the well-doing or ill-doing of the individual persons composing, at a particular moment of time, the nations or the government; these have their future, not in this world, but individually in the world beyond. Thus, if the Jewish writers of apocalypses, failing to find correspondence between well-doing and prosperity in the history of nations, sought compensation in the belief that the correspondence would be established in a future state of mankind, that compensation did not mean that nations now acting righteously would be happy as nations, in that future state, but simply that while now wicked nations prospered, wickedness in that future state would be abolished. So far as *reward* for well-doing in the future life went, that only applied to individuals; if national ill-doing consisted really in the acts of a number of individual rulers, it could be punished only by those rulers being punished individually, either in a discarnate state after death or after a future resurrection or both.

The apocalyptic view was endorsed, as to its main purport by Jesus—a time of trouble and anguish to be expected, and then the coming in glory and power of the Son of Man, the kingdom of God, not established by any human effort but miraculously by God Himself. The apocalyptic view passed to the Christian Church. Its hope differed in this from the hope of contemporary Judaism, that Christians knew who the Messiah to come on the clouds of heaven would be.

The fortunes of individuals and nations, it was said just now, are determined partly by their voluntary actions, partly by natural processes outside their control. The weather may be a principal factor in determining the result of a campaign; an epidemic at a particular moment may affect the future course of history. When God is spoken of as the Lord of history, these natural processes must be supposed to be under His control. If they were not, a wet season might upset God's plans, and He could not direct history as its Lord. Every process in the world has will behind it. In the case of things brought about by human or animal action, the will is that of the individual man or animal, these living creatures having been endowed by God, as part of His purpose in constituting this particular kind of universe, with a certain power of independent action. In the case of all the processes of inanimate matter the only will behind them can be God's, and God's will is always good.[1] The problem offered by the belief that God is the Lord of history is that the operation of these natural laws, governed by no will but His, do not appear to have any adjustment to moral worth or the desires of the spirit; they go on in complete disregard

[1] I need not go into the question whether any matter is really inanimate: some recent philosophers have supposed that the minutest constituents of matter are governed by some sort of mind, and that the regularity of the laws of nature is the regularity of statistics. For the purposes of the argument it is enough to proceed on the ordinary view that the movements of material masses—stars or stones—when once launched, are determined by regular natural laws unaffected by any will, except that of God, who constituted the universe so.

of anything but mechanical uniformity, sometimes accidentally giving an advantage to goodness, but as often as not giving an advantage to wickedness.[1]

If the universe is constituted by God to be such as it is and spirits are here incarnate with their material environment, we can only believe that it is good for spirits, during their incarnation, to live in such a world as this, where matter is governed by its own uniform laws. It is good for them, as part of their discipline in this world, to live under the domination of the iron processes, whose effects they can in some small degree adjust to their purposes through the power of moving the material substance of their bodies and, by means of that, of moving other material masses. But they cannot bring about any break in the material processes; so far as they cannot affect them through their bodily movements, they must submit to them; they must determine their own attitude and conduct in view of events which they cannot alter; soon after three-score years and ten, if not before, their bodies, whatever they may do, will be destroyed by them. If, in many cases, the event which the spirit would desire, the value, moral or æsthetic or utilitarian, for which spirit is concerned is negated, because its realization would involve a break in the iron processes, we must believe that, on the long view, it is better for the spirit that the event or value should, in that particular instance, be negated than that the discipline of living under these processes should be relaxed. They are the rules of the school which we have to be subject to while we are here.

So far as men can bring about events in the material

[1] "Neither the much-hoped-for thaw nor the usual February snowstorms have come to the rescue of the Finns who were desperately resisting almost incessant attacks by vastly superior forces."—*Daily Telegraph*, March 1, 1940.

world which they desire, it is only—apart from action by God, in answer to human prayer—by moving matter in such a way that, according to natural uniform law, the desired result follows. Good men in earlier times have believed that God's action might take the form of producing an event which would not have occurred if material laws had followed their natural course. In battle against the Midianites, for instance, victory, according to natural law, would most probably go to the side on which the larger number of human bodies were driving cutting instruments into bodies on the other side. Gideon, the story says, was ordered by God to reduce his numbers to a handful, so that the victory might be shown to be procured, not according to natural law, but by direct action of God. It came to be an accepted maxim that God could save by many, or by few.[1]

The Israelite tribes had overrun and conquered Palestine. With their spears and swords they had actually killed numbers of the former inhabitants, and it might seem that it was in consequence of this, according to the natural processes of the world, that they had obtained possession of the land. No,

For they got not the land in possession by their own sword,
  Neither did their own arm save them,
But thy right hand and thine arm and the light of thy countenance
  Because thou hadst a favour unto them.[2]

Hence the extreme danger of men's boasting beforehand of what they are going to do, in reliance upon the material means at their disposal. "Woe to them that go down to Egypt for help, and stay on horses; and trust in chariots, because they are many, and in horsemen because they are very strong; but they

[1] 1 Maccabees iii. 18. [2] Psalm xliv. 3.

look not unto the Holy One of Israel, neither seek the Lord!"[1]

Here, again, the Greeks offer a parallel. For them, too, it was dangerous to boast beforehand, because it provoked the Unseen Power to humble him who lifted himself up without remembering his dependence on the Divine. Ajax, when he left home for Troy, said to his father: "Father, with the help of gods even a man of nought might win the mastery: but I, even without their aid, trust to bring that glory within my grasp." "So proud was his vaunt."[2] And the goddess Athena drove him to madness and suicide.

In the Prayer Book which we use to-day the prayer "In the Time of War" calls God "the only giver of victory." Rudyard Kipling in what is perhaps his best known poem, which won the warm approval of religious people in England, wrote:

> For heathen heart that puts her trust
> In reeking tube and iron shard,
> All valiant dust that builds on dust,
> And, guarding, calls not Thee to guard,
> For frantic boast and foolish word—
> Thy Mercy on Thy People, Lord!

The *Recessional* is considered an eminently Christian poem, and it is possible, I believe, to take it in a Christian sense. But in its surface meaning it does not appear to me distinctively Christian. It has close affinity with the sentiments which issued, in the passage just noted, from the "heathen heart" of the poet Sophocles. A great display of power, such as went with the Diamond Jubilee of Queen Victoria, might well, according to ancient Greek feeling, be dangerous; it might provoke the *nemesis* of the gods. It might bring very bad luck, unless you counteracted

[1] Isaiah xxxiii. 1

[2] Sophocles, *Ajax*, 766-9.

the display by some expression of dependence upon the Divine Power. The ancient "heathen" were less disposed than we are to trust to their instruments of bronze and iron, without earnest efforts to conciliate that inscrutable Power.

Can we sincerely say to-day that we do not put our trust in reeking tube and iron shard? We think it all important in this struggle to get the largest number of men we can into the field, and we strain every nerve to multiply aircraft and munitions. Over and over again, when the people are encouraged by the speeches of statesmen and by the national broadcasts to be confident of victory, what is pointed to is the unparalleled strength of our ships of war and the excellence of our airmen. Is this all wrong? Ought we to take Kipling's rebuke simply, and be quite content, so long as our cause is good and we have prayed to God for victory, to go into battle with tubes and shards small in number and inferior in quality? If you understand "put your trust in tube and shard" to mean forecast the likelihood of victory because you have a superior supply of tubes and shards, I think it is quite right to do so. When you have once given up the ancient idea that God can be looked to to bring about results we desire which would not be brought about by the normal operation of natural laws, when you have recognized natural laws to be the school regulations in our present existence, you are bound to forecast the likelihood of this or the other event occurring by supposing that the processes will follow these laws, so far as you know the laws and existing facts. Thus suppose two contending forces are approximately equal in numbers and effective training, you must regard the side which has the superiority in tubes and shards as the more likely to win, and if that happens to be your own side, you are quite right in basing your relative confidence on your tubes and shards. Public speakers and broadcasters are quite right when they tell us to estimate the probability of our beating Germany high, because we have, especially since the new American neutrality legislation, larger supplies of ships and munitions and aircraft. There is nothing impious in such relative trust.

But there is another sense in which Christians must say that it is wrong to put trust in tubes and shards. If you mean that tubes and shards can secure you real good, happiness in the truest sense, then your trust is misplaced. Real good can be secured only by a spiritual condition in harmony with God's will. Victory in war perhaps tubes and shards may secure us, but if victory in war goes with a spiritual condition in the victors out of harmony with God's will, a spirit of pride, hatred and uncharitableness, the victory may be only an evil. There is a verse of the Psalms (Prayer Book version) "He gave them their desire, and sent leanness withal into their soul."[1] That is it. It is only when the result won by tubes and shards is won in subordination to an end of spiritual value, when the victory enables a condition of things to be established in the world in which men are freer for the higher human activities, that the tubes and shards have been instruments for the winning of real good. And this can never happen unless the men who use the tubes and shards care for a great deal more than beating their enemies.

There is something further we have to consider. The most extensive accumulation of the material means for bringing about a desired event only increases the *probability* of its being effected, it cannot give certainty. The result is always determined in part by a number of factors in the natural world,

[1] Psalm cvi. 15.

over which we have no control—the issue of a campaign, for instance, as was said just now, by the weather. Again, beside factors in the material environment, there are the minds and wills of all the people upon whose action the result in part depends—those of the enemy, those of neighbouring peoples who may remain neutral or may join our side or may give help to the enemy. Both these kinds of factors, which it is not in our power to shape to our will, represent what in any enterprise we sometimes speak of as *the chapter of accidents.* It is an inscrutable region out of which may come the most unpleasant surprises. The best-laid plans may be overthrown by them. You never can tell beforehand what is lurking in ambush for you there. That is why it is felt to be dangerous to put over-confidence in your preparations, to boast. Just because that implies a forgetfulness (" Lest we forget ") of the chapter of accidents, that dark Power may be provoked to assert itself and bring all your preparations to nought. Then the more you have boasted, the more foolish you will look. " Provoke," we have said, because peoples have always tended to personalize in some way the chapter of accidents, to attribute to it such resentment as a man of mysterious power might feel at being overlooked. That was what the Greeks meant by the *nemesis* of the gods. " He that sitteth in the heavens shall laugh: the Lord shall have them in derision."[1] And so far as the chapter of accidents has been personalized, men have felt it possible to do something beforehand to win its favour, by sacrifice, by prayer —by self-humiliation, to show that you recognize your dependence upon it, the inadequacy of all preparation you may make. Such recognition will please it.

[1] Psalm ii. 4.

Christians too believe that the chapter of accidents is ruled by God. That chapter, we have just seen, consists of factors of two kinds—conditions and events in the world of inanimate matter, the minds and wills of other men. Conditions and events in the world of inanimate matter are brought about, as was said just now, so far as they are not brought about by human or animal volition, solely by the will of God. It is a more difficult problem to say in what sense, or to what extent, the wills of men are ruled by God.

To consider first the conditions and events in the world of inanimate matter, so far as the result of any enterprise upon which we embark is determined by them, we can say only that our efforts had that result because God willed the material conditions to be such as they were. The unceasing rain which affected the dreadful Passchendaele campaign of 1917 was, as legal terminology recognizes, an "act of God." No doubt it is a problem how God makes events in the material world fit in with what He sees to be good at that moment for the human spirits affected by them, with His direction of human history. So far as I can see, either events in the material world, so far as they are not interfered with by human or animal volition, follow a sequence determined by the invariable laws of matter from the beginning, and then we must believe that the distribution of matter in space was originally determined by God precisely so as to bring about the required result at a particular spot on the earth's surface at a particular date, or we must believe that the processes of the material world are not absolutely rigid, but are modified, as they go on, by God to fit in with conditions brought about by the free wills of men. Which view is the right one need not be discussed here. All that is necessary for our purposes is to recognize that somehow or other events in the material world are ordered by God as He sees to be good for the spirits of men. Otherwise, if God exists at all and cares for men, we should have to suppose that when men are hurt by any physical accident beyond their control, God could only say, " I am very sorry; I could not help it; I never foresaw that things would fall out like that."

When we come to the part of human will in determining events, the problem of God's rule of history is a much more complicated one. In regard to the processes of inanimate matter, God's will is already done on earth as it is in heaven because behind these processes there is no will but God's and therefore no possible opposition to His will. But He has conferred on man the power of acting in opposition to His will, and in this respect the Lord's Prayer implies that God's will is not at present done on earth. If, therefore, the result of a conflict between two peoples is in part determined by the action of the men engaged on both sides, and God allows these men to act in opposition to His will, how can we be sure that the result corresponds with God's will? If it does not correspond with His will, then the whole of history may take a course not corresponding with His will, and His Lordship of history is reduced to very little, a phrase. Let us suppose the victory won, and then ask how God can be declared to have been " the only giver " of it. It was determined in part by events in the material environment, in part by the voluntary choices on both sides to act in this way or in that. The events in the material environment we have seen to be determined (except in so far as men can affect them by their bodily movements) by no will but God's, and if their share in producing the victory was so predominant that the enemy could not possibly have won whatever he did, if, for instance, he had been consumed by fire from heaven as the enemies of Jerusalem are conceived to be in Revelation (xx. 9), there would be no question of anyone being the giver of that victory but God. But in the victories won in the course of history the result is only partly determined by the material environment. The rain of Passchendaele would not by itself have determined the result of the campaign without voluntary actions of fighting and endurance on both sides. If the victory is bestowed by an act of God, how can it at the same time be due to the action of human wills which are all more or less contrary to God's will?

We may answer, with the Prayer Book, that God "orders the unruly wills and affections of sinful men," and while people who pride themselves on being scientific tell us that it is wrong to imagine God's ever modifying material processes in a way different from the course prescribed by uniform law, there cannot reasonably be the same objection to thinking of God's modifying the mental and volitional processes of men, because the operations of mind and will cannot be shown to follow unvarying law in the way the processes of matter apparently do. There is no "breach of natural law," if God causes a man to will in a certain way, as there would be if he caused a mountain to move into the midst of the sea. So far then as the victory is determined by the actions of men on this side and the other, there is not the same difficulty, from the scientific point of view, in believing that He caused those on the winning side to will those actions which procured victory and prevented those on the losing side from willing the actions which would have secured the victory for them. But if objection to such a view does not arise from the scientific standpoint, an objection may be raised from the standpoint of a philosophy which attaches importance to human free will. If the wills and affections of men are ordered in this way by God, how can they ever be "unruly"? When an effect is produced by the evil will of men, how can it be regarded as caused by God? The most obvious factor in producing some victories is the evil will of men.

It is to be noted in this connexion that when anything brought about by human effort is regarded as due to God, this is in proportion to the extent to which the chapter of accidents counts in the result. When an effect is produced by man's initiating a material process which, according to natural law, is pretty certain to follow a particular course, the result is not usually regarded as bestowed by an act of Divine grace. If workmen are blasting a cliff, they set going the process which leads to the explosion and it never occurs to them, when the explosion occurs and the rock falls, to kneel down and thank God that the process has had its expected termination, as men do kneel down sometimes and thank God for victory in war. In war the chapter of accidents, which may affect the result, is far more extensive than in the work of blasting rocks. So far as that chapter includes material processes, the weather and so on, it is no more and no less governed by God than the process which leads from the application of a match to an explosion. But the point is that the workman knows beforehand with fair certainty what the process which follows the application of the match will be, whereas the element of ignorance beforehand, as to the material conditions which will affect the issue of a campaign, is very great. Both processes are willed entirely by God in so far as they follow natural law. It may be an act of man's evil will which applies the match, but the process once started follows a law which God's will has imposed upon matter and consistently carries out. There are cases of victory in war in which one side has such a material superiority that the likelihood of its purposes being frustrated by the chapter of accidents is as small as the likelihood of the result which the rock-blaster expects failing to occur. A cynic has said that God is always on the side of the big battalions, and in a sense this is true. The material superiority of one side may be such that its victory could be prevented only by God's so deflecting the process from the course it would follow according to natural law as to constitute a "miracle." And it is apparently God's general will that there should be no relaxation of that law, so that, when a process is initiated by the evil will of man, it follows its natural course even if the result is in itself evil. In Tasmania in the nineteenth century men of two races were pitted against each other: on one side were the white settlers with their modern fire-arms, on the other the Tasmanian natives who were still in the Stone Age. The victory of the white settlers was so complete that by the end of the century there was not a single Tasmanian left. Was God the "only giver" of that victory? The same question applies to other victories where the sides are more nearly matched, but still unequally matched. The Germans in September, 1939, won a rapid victory over the Poles, having a marked superiority of numbers and mechanical apparatus on their side. May that victory be ascribed to God alone?

Are those who have engaged in war for a just cause wrong if they pray to God for victory and thank God for victory, should it come? I do not think they are wrong. The course of this world, whose material processes are governed, so far as we can trace them, by a natural law which takes no account of good and evil—the environment most fitting, we must believe, to be the school and training-ground for beings endowed with the power of choice between good and evil—does not, as a matter of fact, bring only evil to man; it brings him, all along, a great deal of good. It continually presents him with things to make him happy, the pleasantness and beauty of much that he feels and sees, the opportunities for increasing knowledge, the order, justice and freedom actualized to a greater or less extent in human society, the joy of love and friendship. True, it brings also to men a great deal of evil—bodily pain, narrowing of opportunity, humiliation in subjection to tyranny, ugly defacement and squalor of the immediate environment, the experience of human unkindness, of human treachery. The elements of good and evil are variously mixed for different men; some live their lives under conditions of misery, some in predominantly happy circumstances; but there is no life which has not some visiting of joy in it, and no life entirely free from pain and distress. If God is the Lord of history, He must be Lord of those individual lives whose sum total constitutes history, and then it must be believed that the circumstances, pleasant or unpleasant, in which each individual, coming into the world, finds himself placed, must be those which God sees to be best for the fashioning of this particular soul by the way in which the person deals in his voluntary decisions with the problem set him. The evils which befall him without any fault of his own come then within the design of God for the earthly life of this soul, and are in that sense to be taken as God's loving will. But ought we to regard evils as sent us by God in the same sense in which we so regard the good things which life brings? The answer, I think, is No. The good things are good in themselves and express God's love, in bestowing them, as they are; the evil things in themselves are evil, but they may form part of a whole whose totality is better, with those evils in it, than it could be if they were not there. If, for instance, there were no possibility of man's voluntarily choosing evil, there would be no possibility of his voluntarily choosing good, and the result would be only a creature with the perfection of a machine, which is of less worth than the perfection of a free spirit. If there were no pain in life, there would be no possibility of the human spirit's developing that specific character which is got by the way it deals with pain. But the choosing of evil is in itself nothing but an evil; pain in itself is nothing but an evil. It is therefore not reasonable to thank God for the pain, or to see in the pain by itself an expression of His Love; but it is reasonable to thank God for that totality of life which makes the pain the means to a higher good than could be bestowed without it, and to see in the pain, as *a part of that totality*, an expression of God's love.

Now apply this to victory in war won by those who have the right on their side. When we survey the victories won throughout history we cannot see any Divine purpose giving victory always to the better cause. Whatever God's design for world history may be, it plainly allows of victory in war often falling to the evil power. In this respect, too, life shows a mixture and variation of good and evil. But the victory of a just cause is in itself a good, and the victory of a bad cause in itself an evil. The victory of a bad cause may lead in the end to a higher spiritual good in the world, if the people affected by it react to it in the right way. It might, for instance, lead to a searching of heart and a new impulse to do everything possible to obviate such evil occurring again. If so, it would be right to thank God for the totality of events which included the victory of the bad cause as an essential part of it, but it would not be reasonable to thank God for the victory of the bad cause by itself. It would, on the other hand, be right to thank God for the victory of a just cause by itself; that, by itself, would be an instalment of good.

The question how, if God allows evil men often to have their way, in conquest as in other things, it is possible for His design, as Lord of history, to be carried through, can so far as I can see, be answered only on the supposition that while God allows a certain scope to human will, and so saves its freedom, that scope is strictly circumscribed. Evil men are allowed by God to will or to perform many things, but never those things which would impair the carrying out of His design. Thus when a victory won is ascribed to God it is because that mass of factors unknown beforehand which were included in the chapter of accidents proved to be such as to allow the victors to realize their purpose, and, inasmuch as those factors included the wills of the enemy, and the enemy, if they had willed certain courses of action might have secured the victory, God did not allow the enemy to think of those courses of action or, at any rate, to will them. At that point, one might say, their minds were, without their knowing it, struck with paralysis.

As we look along the course of human history it may be difficult to prove progress on the total account, because progress in one respect often goes with retrogression in another respect and advance at one period is often followed by a set-back in the next period. Yet this thing may strike us. Good is never allowed to perish altogether. Something of the good is always kept in being through the worst epochs, and later on revives again in power. The Church may become torpid, corrupt; Christians may be persecuted, reduced in numbers; yet the gates of Hades never quite prevail against the Church.[1] When the army of Christ moves behind its standards, slow, full of misgivings, thin in number, the heavenly Commander sends the champions at whose word "the people which had lost the way rallies once more."[2]

Thus a Catholic poet of the nineteenth century saw the human race as a herd always drifting to the abyss and yet always held back from utter destruction by the hidden operation of God.

Nathess, discern'd may be
By listeners at the doors of destiny
The fly-wheel swift and still
Of God's incessant will,
Mighty to keep in bound, tho' powerless to quell,
The amorous and vehement drift of man's herd to hell.[3]

If the victory of a just cause is in itself a good for which we ought to thank God, then it is reasonable to pray for it. Of course various objections have been raised to the idea of praying for anything at all. It would not be possible to go into them here; there is a plentiful discussion of them in current religious literature, and anybody who thinks it worth while to know what Christian thinkers have said on the subject can certainly do so. Here, one may take it for granted that it is reasonable for a man to lay before

[1] Matthew xvi. 18.

[2] "L'esercito di Cristo, che sì caro
Costò a riarmar, dietro all' insegna
Si movea tardo, suspiccioso e raro:
Quando lo Imperador che sempre regna
Provvide alla milizia ch'era in forse,
Per sola grazia, non per esser degna;
E, com' è detto, a sua sposa soccorse
Con due campioni, al cui fare, al cui dire
Lo popol disviato si raccorse."
Dante, *Paradiso* xii. 37-45.

[3] Coventry Patmore, "Crest and Gulf" in *The Unknown Eros.*

God in prayer his desire for something which appears to him good.[1] If the victory of a just cause is really a good, then it would be included among the good things for which it is reasonable to pray. And what applies to prayer for other things which seem to us good applies also to this. What we pray for may not be granted. We may be wrong in supposing the thing we desire to be good. In the case of victory, the cause which we believe to be the just cause may not really be just; or, if we are right in believing it to be just, it may come within God's design to allow the evil cause on this occasion to triumph. But if we are not going to pray for what we believe to be good, because we may be mistaken in believing it to be good, then we can never pray for anything.

One objection has been often raised to praying for victory by people who seem to think they are saying something clever when they are only saying something silly. It is ridiculous, they say, to ask God to give our side victory because the other side is equally asking Him to give them victory, and so the two prayers cancel out. This would be apt only if Christians regarded prayer as a kind of natural or magical force directed upon God as upon an inanimate body. But each side appeals to God as Some One who cares for justice, because each side believes its own cause to be the just one. One side or the other must be mistaken. The two prayers are not therefore analogous; one is for the victory of the right, one for the victory of wrong, and if man's judgment about right and wrong is very fallible, God is here the Judge. To say that it is ridiculous to ask God for victory because the other side asks God for victory is precisely as if we should maintain that there is no such thing as

[1] One may refer, for instance, to the composite volume, *Concerning Prayer*. (Macmillan.)

justice at all, no such thing as right and wrong, because in every conflict both sides appeal to the principles of justice and maintain that these principles support their contention, and not that of the enemy. Prayer for victory would no doubt be absurd, if we asked God to give our side the victory because it is ours, not because it is (as we believe) the side of justice.

When the material superiority is very great on one side in the conflict, as in the case of the white colonists and the natives of Tasmania, it is not probable that boasting and self-assurance will provoke God, as the heathens supposed, to punish the *hybris* by signal overthrow. It is more likely that the stronger side will carry out their purpose unchecked. The stronger side in such a case could hardly be prevented from carrying out their purpose except by some miraculous modification of the processes of nature which it is apparently God's will not to allow in the present state of things. Yet the boasting and self-assurance are no less dangerous than the heathen supposed, though dangerous in another way. For all true good (as was said just now) man is utterly dependent upon God. Any boasting and self-assurance which denies that dependence implies a spiritual attitude which alienates from God, and however successful men may be in carrying out their purposes, that alienation means that they miss in this life the highest good of man, and will find the bitterness of it, if not here, in the life beyond. A recent much-read book seems to me to furnish an example of precisely that kind of boasting which is farther away than the "heathen heart" of the ancient Greeks was from the right spirit. Mr. Clarence Streit in his *Union Now*, has a passage which is made the more noticeable by being the peroration with which a principal section of his book concludes (page 320): "Man has on earth no one but Man to help him,[1] and what a mighty, what a generous, what a kindly and abiding and dependable friend and liberator is Man to Man. Man has already wrought miracles of Man by Man for Man. These are great and they are but a hint of those that will be done when our Union opens Man's vast future."

The book in which this passage occurs is an argument for the political federation of democratic states with which any believer in God may heartily concur. It was therefore all the more gratuitous to introduce a passage of constructive atheism. It was the more inept inasmuch as Mr. Streit presumably desires to get as much support as he can from people of all shades of opinion, and to introduce matter which could be only offensive to Christians and Theists, who after all do form a considerable section of the community, was needlessly to queer his own pitch. Probably Mr. Streit's outbreak is typical of the "Humanism" which has had a vogue in America. Even atheists of finer perceptions might, I think, be repelled by this trumpeting assurance in its Philistine insensibility to the tragic element in human nature and the questionable shadows on the future of Man.

[1] Contrast the phrase in our Prayer Book, "For there is none other that fighteth for us, save only Thou, O God."

CHAPTER V

THE END OF HISTORY

So we Christians look at this process of nineteen hundred years which have gone by since the great hope lit up by the Resurrection of the Lord first shone —a process in which good and evil, light and darkness, have mingled and alternated in a way too complicated for man to trace up to this year A.D. 1940, when the more limited hope which our generation had cherished, of making the world in certain respects better, has been confused by our seeing men's evil will rise up armed over a great part of the earth and the future take in forecast cloudy shapes of fear. And I come back to the question with which Chapter II ended: What are we to say about the Christian hope now?

One thing we can say at once for certain, something which must be admitted by everybody, whether they are Christians or adherents of some other religion or materialists. The process of mankind's history on earth is bound sooner or later to come to an end. Life cannot continue on this planet for ever. It may come to a sudden end by some cosmic cataclasm; it may peter out by degrees. If it is not ended by a cataclasm then some millions of years hence, perhaps before, material conditions on the globe will become more and more difficult for the living beings upon it— whether from the globe losing its moisture or from decrease in the sun's heat or in some other way. Suppose by that time men have accumulated a much larger scientific knowledge than they have to-day, the human race may by ingenious expedients prolong the battle against circumstances becoming ever more and more adverse. But it will be a losing battle, just as the battle of an individual to prolong his bodily life by the inventions of medical science against the process of decay may succeed in adding some years to his life, but is all the same a losing battle and ends in death. These last phases of the history of the race, as one by one the material things it needs for its well-being fail, are likely (if we leave out of account the possibility of a "miraculous" change of earthly conditions) to be distressful ones—no earthly Paradise. Then a time will come when all life on the globe is extinct, and the globe will continue to wheel in space, a dead world, like the moon to-day. If mankind has no future except on this planet, all the millions who have lived here will have ceased utterly to exist. In that universal death for unmeasured time to come, it will make no difference at all what the history of man has been; whether we succeed for the moment in making a better world or not, it will all come to the same in the end.

The belief that mankind is destined to that complete extinction is compatible, I think, only with an atheistic view of the universe. For if you suppose that God exists independently of man, then you must suppose that for all time after that death of the globe God goes on existing as Spirit with no longer any of those human spirits in fellowship with Him, for whom He was believed to care so much. All that spiritual intercourse between the Supreme Spirit and the created human spirits will have been abolished for ever. If God is such as we believe, this does not seem likely. Or if you say that God also will cease to exist when the human race dies, then whatever it was which existed before under the name of God was something so different from what Christians and Theists mean by God that to call it by the same name is absurd. Thus it seems clear that if God will exist as eternal Spirit after the globe perishes, the human spirits with whom He has entered into communion will also live as undying spirits after the globe has perished.

If this is so, it makes a great difference to the way in which we regard the course of the world around us—the national interests, the social movements, the achievements and losses of our generation, the wars and desolations. Looked at from the standpoint of earth, the nation, the society, seems to endure, the individuals composing it at any moment to perish.

> Time, like an ever-rolling stream,
> Bears all its sons away;
> They fly forgotten, as a dream
> Dies at the opening day.

"Even as are the generations of leaves such are those likewise of men," another ancient poet has said; "the leaves that be the wind scattereth on the earth, and the forest buddeth and putteth forth more again, when the season of spring is at hand; so of the generations of men one putteth forth and another ceaseth."[1] England abides, but each individual Englishman has only his little day, and, with few exceptions, is no more than a shadowy name, if as much, to his own descendants a hundred years later. That is the aspect which things present to the common eye. But, according to Christian belief, it is the individual who endures and England that, sooner or later, will perish.

The direction in which to look for the future of mankind is not along the course of history on this

[1] Homer, *Iliad* vi. 146-9. Lang, Leaf and Myers' Translation. (Macmillan.)

planet. It is obliquely *across* the historical process, not along it, that the millions of human spirits are always streaming. This life is only a platform where they remain for a moment on their journey to the unseen world. If you look for the sea towards which the streaming of generations is set, it is out there, beyond bodily death; the future for them lies out there. The groups which seem so permanent, in contrast with the perishing individuals—the family, the society, the nation—are merely frames within which during their time on earth human spirits are brought together to be exercised in different kinds of fellowship. The spirits, when their time of learning here is over, pass on, and the frames, when they have served their turn, will some day be broken up.

There is only one society, partially manifested on earth, which is an eternal frame, which continues, as a society, in the world beyond death; and that is the Mystical Body of Christ.

Had one asked a Christian in the first century what the future was to which he looked forward, he would have said that it was the gathering together in the wonder-world of all the members of Christ's Body, immune for ever more from death, in a perfect union of intercourse with the Lord Jesus, in a fellowship, inconceivable now, of all the members of His Body with each other. He would perhaps have added that he expected this to come about within his own, or the next generation, when all the dead in Christ would rise and those members of the community who were alive and remained would be caught up, together with them, in the clouds, to meet the Lord in the air, and so would be for ever with the Lord. The early Christian's expectation of this event in the near future proved to be a mistake, but, apart from that, the early Christian's hope, as I have just defined it, is precisely what the Church still professes to hope for to-day—the union of the whole body of those animated by the Spirit of Christ "with the Lord" in perfect fellowship and for ever beyond the reach of death. No state of mankind on this planet under the present processes of the physical world could ever fulfil that hope. It is obviously other-worldly—*jenseits*, as the Germans say, "on the side beyond." A union of the whole Body of Christ, of all who in any age have been animated by His Spirit, could never exist except beyond death and under conditions which, in contrast with the conditions of our space and time, would constitute a wonder-world.

That is still the hope of the Church to-day. But the lapse of nineteen centuries leaves us with the question how far we can take the apocalyptic imagery in which the hope was clothed for the early Church to correspond with actual future events. Some people think it quite a simple affair to say, "Of course, those are symbols which we cannot take literally to-day, even if they were literally understood by Christians in the first century." But it is really not such an easy matter to say how far the symbolism goes. No doubt many people have gone absurdly wrong in the direction of literalness. In my youth I knew a clergyman —let us call him Mr. Wilkinson[1]—who was a fervent believer in those schemes of future events which Evangelicals commonly thought they could extract from Biblical prophecies. A friend staying with him —his vicarage was on the coast—was kept awake one foggy night by a fog-horn continually sounding at sea. He spoke of it at breakfast the next morning, and asked Mr. Wilkinson whether he too had been troubled by it. "No," Mr. Wilkinson said, "no, I

[1] "A Mr. Wilkinson, a clergyman"—the line Tennyson made up to parody Wordsworth.

did not hear it," and then added, looking very solemn, "If I *had* heard it, I should have thought it was the Last Trump." "My dear Wilkinson," his friend, who was touched with modernism, exclaimed, "you cannot really suppose the Last Trump to be like a foghorn! Surely it is a symbol for a general awakening of conscience, or something of that kind. You cannot think that it is literally a trumpet of brass!" Mr. Wilkinson was perplexed for a moment; then his face lit up, "I think," he said, "perhaps it may be *silver*."

Well, we can all see that there is a great deal in the apocalyptic imagery which it is absurd to take literally. But what many people fail to see is that you may equally give up the essential Christian hope if you carry the theory of symbolism too far. The real may for you evaporate into a mist. There is a point where you have to stop and say, "This I believe to be literally true itself, not to be merely a figurative way of representing something else which is true." If what you took to be the truth behind the symbol turns out, on closer inspection, to be itself only a symbol for a truth still more remote, and then when you try to get to that truth, that in turn is found to be a symbol, you may never get to solid truth at all. Probably most of the people who say most glibly, "Of course the traditional Christian ideas of the coming kingdom of God are to be taken as symbols," would admit, if you pressed them, that if everything in the tradition, absolutely everything, were to be taken as only symbolic, you would be left with nothing in the end to distinguish such a view from pure agnosticism. As a matter of fact, one form of agnosticism which had considerable vogue some years ago, Vaihinger's interpretation of the Kantian philosophy, did proceed upon this very supposition, that all that men had taken for truths were only symbols. It was labelled the philosophy of "Als ob," "As if."

If then there is a pitfall on each side of the road—that of understanding literally what ought to be understood symbolically and that of understanding symbolically what ought to be understood literally—it is a question of some difficulty where you are to draw the line; it is futile to try to ride off with some facile generality about prophetic imagery being symbolic. No doubt some variety of opinion is inevitable among present-day Christians as to where the line comes. Each one of us is likely to find that the line drawn by this one or the other of his fellow-Christians departs more or less from his own, either in the direction of literalism or in the direction of symbolism.

The Christian hope has to do with two kinds of eschatology—if one must use the technical theological term for "doctrine about the last things." One kind has to do with the destiny of individuals beyond bodily death; the other has to do with the consummation to which human history on this planet is moving. If I put down what seems to me personally the element of essential truth and the element of symbol in traditional doctrine on these two subjects, those who read this may see how far they agree, or where they are led to make a different division.

The New Testament doctrine about the destiny of the individual beyond bodily death is that, if he has been, during his earthly life, in fellowship with Christ he will be "with Christ" when he passes from the body,[1] and that, in any case, everyone must "stand before the judgment seat of God,"[2] or, in an equiva-

[1] 2 Corinthians v. 6-8; Philippians i. 23.

[2] Romans xiv. 10. The true reading is here pretty certainly "judgment seat of God," not "judgment seat of Christ," as in our Authorized Version. The fact that in 2 Corinthians "judgment seat of Christ" is used as apparently equivalent in meaning is of crucial significance for St. Paul's belief about the Lord Jesus.

lent phrase, "appear before the judgment seat of Christ."[1] The figure borrowed from the tribunals of earth is obviously symbolic; it is not to be supposed that Christ sits on a literal throne and that the person, after death, stands before that throne with two feet upon material ground. But it would seem to me fatal to carry the symbolism so far as to deny that the person who passes through death does, in some mode or other, really experience the presence of Christ, of the same Person who on earth was known as Jesus the Nazarene, now recognized as bearing the irresistible authority of God, and, as a consequence of that Presence, sees, as he never had seen before, the real quality of the life he lived on earth and of the character he has made for himself by it, without any possibility of excuse or self-deception—an experience in which there may be keen pain and shame even for those to whom the presence of the Lord brings at the same time an overwhelming joy.[2]

As the real experience of a particular person, this would be an *event*. The reason which leads some people to wish to dissolve into symbolism any belief in life after death is, I think, an unwillingness to believe in any events outside those of earthly life. An event occupying a point of time seems to them somehow of inferior dignity to the apprehension of a timeless value, and they are fain to translate all language about the personal life beyond death into some such apprehension of value within a man's earthly life—the only life he will ever have. An event has necessarily some place in time, so that, if you believe that any event is possible beyond death, you must believe

[1] 2 Corinthians v. 10.

[2] There is, I think, nothing self-contradictory in supposing the co-existence at the same time in a person's spirit of joy and pain. The souls in Purgatory are, according to Dante, "*contenti* nel fuoco." (*Inferno* i. 118, 119.)

that time continues in some sort beyond death. It need not be time having the same measures as our earthly time, but it must involve temporal succession.[1] The experience beyond death, if an event, must stand in a temporal relation to earthly experience; it would be definitely *after* earthly experience, and not before it, or contemporaneous with it. Now the same people who do not like giving events high spiritual dignity, dislike also admitting the reality of time, and supposing that there can be any sort of time in the unseen world. This hostility to events and to time seems to me quite unjustified. It is plainly incompatible with the Christian view of the world which gives supreme importance to events in time—the Incarnation, the Death, the Resurrection of the Divine Being at definite dates in history. It seems quite inconsistent to believe that Christ lived and died, not as a symbolic myth, but in a series of actual events, and to be shocked if anyone believes in a future meeting of Christ and individual men, as a real event, and say, " Oh, of course, that can be only symbolical." I think we have to recognize that value is not lowered or coarsened by being embodied in events; it is only when embodied in events that it is real.

A question is raised by the traditional doctrine of the Resurrection of the Body. It is not clear when St. Paul speaks of our standing before the judgment seat of God, whether he is thinking of the discarnate person doing so immediately after death or the person reclad with his body doing so at the Last Day. The later Christian tradition, as we have seen, assumed a double judgment, and it is no doubt difficult for us

[1] I think one must distinguish between the order of temporal succession, which seems to me something real, and the *measure* of time, the relative swiftness or slowness with which events follow each other, which may be simply a matter of subjective apprehension.

to make sense of this view. Most modern Christians do not think that the Resurrection of the Body means a reassembling of the identical particles of matter which constituted the old body: they follow rather a suggestion of St. Paul as to a "heavenly body" distinct from the earthly body with which the righteous after death may be clothed.[1] What is important, they insist, is to believe that in the life beyond the person is furnished with ampler means of perception, communication and self-expression, than are given him by his material body here. Those means, whatever they may be, constitute the heavenly body. But, if this is so, there is no reason why the person should not be clothed with the heavenly body immediately after death, while the discarded vesture of earthly life decays in the ground. There is no reason why he should wait for any further resurrection at the Last Day.

Perhaps it is allowable to regard the picture of a future Return of Jesus upon the clouds and the gathering to Him of all members, dead and living, of His Body, as a symbolic representation of the meeting between the Lord and the human person which takes place at each individual's passage from this world, the "General Resurrection" being, not an event at the end of human history on the planet, but a continuous event all along the course of human history, at the side, as it were, of earthly history. The Return of Christ is then indeed near, as the unseen world is all the time near to us, and we may pass out of this world into that world at any moment—a step, and we are in it. The essential thing in the Christian hope is the gathering together of the whole community "with Christ" in a condition free from those

[1] 2 Corinthians v. 1-4.

limitations imposed by the earthly body and the laws of earthly space and time upon fellowship with Christ and with one another. But this gathering together is going on all the time, as each member of Christ passes from this world to join the great "company of heaven"—a company of spirits, discarnate but not unembodied. And St. Paul's phrase about "meeting the Lord in the air" may represent something which really happens when a person dies. Christ may indeed come to meet the discarnate spirit. I have known several cases of persons—an old man, a child, a manual worker—indicating just before death that they "saw the Lord." Of course, such testimony cannot prove that what they believed was true to anyone who thinks it unlikely, and I should never put it forward as having the value of proof; but if, on your general view of things, you do not think it unlikely, such testimony may have value for your personal conviction. Such a view, extending "the Resurrection and the Judgment" to a continuous event along the side of history, gets rid of the difficulty of the double judgment in the traditional view.

But there remains the question, what is the end to which human history on this planet is moving? Granting that a kingdom of God on earth, without an irruption of the wonder-world, could never be a fulfilment of the Christian hope, because it would be a fellowship only of the generations of men alive on earth at one time, not a gathering of the whole Body of Christ, it is conceivable that a state of things might some day exist on the planet in which men generally would be led by the Spirit of Christ and would love each other, the moral evils of present-day society would be done away, and the physical evils which now afflict man very much reduced by greater scientific knowledge. Such a state of things might be described as a relative "Kingdom of God," though it would have to end with the ultimate extinction of life on the planet, and the final stages of man's struggle with physical circumstances would be probably distressful ones, however near perfection the spiritual temper of those last generations of mankind might be. But such a state of things is conceivable, and we may even imagine it extended over more than the thousand years of early Christian Chiliasm.

The term Chiliasm, as commonly used, covers any expectation of such an earthly kingdom of God. The idea is not in favour with theologians: Chiliasm is even used as a term to express depreciation and reproach. An earthly millennium is dismissed as a gross unspiritual idea. This is very odd. Whether there is any reason to expect an earthly reign of Christ or not, unspiritual the idea can hardly be. If it is not unspiritual to believe, as a fact of great religious importance, that Christ lived an actual human life on earthly soil nineteen hundred years ago, how can it be unspiritual to believe that He will dwell again upon earth two thousand years hence, or a hundred thousand years hence, or whatever number of years it may be? If it is not unspiritual to believe that He manifested Himself as alive and present, after the Crucifixion, to Peter and to a gathering of five hundred brethren at the beginning of the Church's earthly story, how can it be unspiritual to believe that He will manifest Himself as alive and present to all the men who will be on earth at the end of the Church's earthly story? If indeed the hope of an earthly kingdom of God is offered as a substitute for the hope of a union of the Body of Christ in heaven, that is a great lowering of the outlook. But with the early Church the earthly millennium was not an alternative to the union of the redeemed in heaven;

it was a lesser hope which was cherished in addition to the greater one.

But even if the idea of an earthly millennium cannot be dismissed as unspiritual, it may still be asked whether there is any ground for expecting it. The great body of the Church soon abandoned the idea, and adopted the supposition that earthly history would be abruptly terminated by a fiery destruction of the globe, conditions on earth growing worse rather than better towards the end, and that the union of the redeemed in heaven remained as the great consummation for eternity.

It is curious to think how on the day on which I am writing this—Advent Sunday, 1939—" Modern Churchmen " among the clergy who believe themselves to hold the truly *scientific* view, because they have eliminated the miraculous from their faith, will have to read out in church the Collect which says—" that in the last day, when he shall come again in his glorious majesty to judge both the quick and the dead, we may rise to the life immortal." That would seem to imply an irruption of the wonder-world some day to occur, which will not only interfere with the processes of this world, but bring them, so far as the human race is concerned, to an end. How, it may be asked, can anyone really believe that such a stupendous event will occur, and boggle at some incidental miracles of the past? Perhaps they would say that they do not believe such an event will ever occur; they are merely using the traditional language, and that language is " symbolical." Symbolical of what? What do they think the real event is or will be, which the language shadows forth in a figure? Could they indicate any real event or experience to which such language could be implied without huge incongruity?

And yet it may be that the supposition of a catastrophic sudden destruction of the globe, and the removal of all remaining human persons into the state beyond death, in which they undergo the Divine Judgment, is reconcilable with a view which repudiates any miraculous interferences with the processes of this world.

One has only to suppose that some conjunction of events in stellar space brings about a disturbance of the solar system and a destruction of the earth, which I suppose astronomers with our present knowledge could hardly pronounce to be impossible. The discarnate spirits of all men then living on the planet would meet with Christ, as all other discarnate spirits, during the ages past, have done, and undergo His judgment, taking their place accordingly in the eternal world of re-embodied spirits. If this is what the end of human history will really be, the traditional imagery of the Last Day, the dissolution of the present world in fire, the Resurrection and Judgment, is a fair presentation of it. The destruction of the globe would be a wholly natural catastrophe; the Judgment on those whose earthly bodies were destroyed and their being clothed with the "bodies" suitable to the eternal state, as events belonging to the other world, would no more imply any interference with the processes of this world than the experience now of persons after death interferes with the processes of this world. Since life on the globe is certain to end somehow, it might be thought a preferable supposition that it would end suddenly by such a cataclasm, when physical conditions on the globe make a happy life for mankind still possible, rather than by a gradual losing battle against conditions growing ever worse and worse. For so far as one can see, there is no third alternative, the end of life on the globe must come in one of those two ways.

But, if one recognizes that the hope of an earthly millennium before the final cataclasm was soon given up by the Christian Church, that the idea is therefore no essential part of Christian belief, can we say that Chiliasm is incompatible with Christian belief? I do not think we can. If we ourselves are disposed to return to this belief of the first generation of Christians, I do not see that we can be proved wrong. The belief seems, for one thing, to accord better than any other with the Lord's Prayer "Thy kingdom come: Thy will be done on earth as it is in heaven." The doing of God's will on earth is spoken of as something distinct from its being done in heaven, and as something which is to be prayed for. The words may be reconciled with the view which subsequently became traditional—the view that there will never be a kingdom of God on earth, but only the perfection of the Divine Community in heaven—if you take "on earth" as a symbolical phrase for human society and regard the prayer as destined to be fulfilled by such a union of redeemed mankind in heaven beyond death. But that perhaps is rather to strain the meaning. There are, however, three possible views, not two only. There is the prevalent view that Chiliasm is wrong, that there certainly will not be any earthly millennium before the final cataclasm; there is the view that there certainly will be an earthly millennium, because the Book of Revelation says so, and that book is inspired in all its statements—a view common in Evangelical circles; and there is a third view, that an earthly millennium is not a certainty, but a possibility, something which may come about if men go the right way to procure it.

There are two ways in which we can conceive its coming about. According to the belief of those early Christians who expected it, it was not to be procured by any human effort; it was to be established abruptly by a manifestation of Christ in power. Jerusalem was not to be built by man in any "green and pleasant land," but would descend out of heaven from God. If we believe that the appearances of Jesus to His disciples after the Resurrection were real manifestations of a living Person exalted to omnipotence[1]—and all Christians do profess to believe that, even those who do not believe in the reanimation of the earthly body of Jesus and the story of the Empty Tomb—then it seems altogether inconsistent to deny the possibility, or even likelihood, of a future manifestation of Jesus on earth, only this time to all men, and with such a putting forth of irresistible power that all opposition of men of evil will is crushed by it, and an earthly kingdom of God established, for so long as human life continues afterwards upon the globe.

The other way in which a kingdom of God on earth might come about is by a gradual process of work and prayer, pushed forward by men of faith, little by little, through a long series of generations. In that way Jerusalem would be built by men, though not without Divine help, by men who did not "cease from mental fight." This is the view of the Armistice Day preacher and very many people to-day. It is quite different, as will be seen, from the early Christian view. It has no warrant in the Old or in the New Testament. But this is not necessarily to say that it is untrue. It is possible to argue: "The early Christians were, we now know, mistaken in one respect, in regard to the *length of time* to elapse before the coming of God's kingdom in power. If so, they may have been mistaken in another respect also—in regard to the *mode*

[1] "All power is given unto me in heaven and earth." Matthew xxviii. 18.

in which the kingdom was ordained to come. What was going to be a long and gradual process they saw, foreshortened, as it were, from one end, as a single great event in the future. Experience of God's ways, of the gradual evolution of mankind in the past, has taught us better now." If this is the true view, then there will be definite progress in the future, even if it is difficult to prove progress in the first nineteen centuries of Christian history. Things will be advanced " little by little," as the broadcast sermon said, by the operation of spiritual forces. Or one should say rather " may be advanced," and the progress in this case would not be any automatic process, but one which went forward by rightly directed voluntary action on the part of men. The earthly kingdom of God would be a possibility, if men, a certain number of men, throughout a series of generations acted rightly, but would never come, if men acted wrong. In this case, as in many others, God would leave it an open choice to men, whether they obeyed Him or not, and they would reap the fruit of their decision accordingly.

Now, with whatever degree of assurance or doubt we may regard the prospect of a kingdom of God on earth in the future, it seems that we must act on the supposition of its possibility, if once we have admitted the possibility that any action of ours can make the world better. We are bound then to make the world good to the utmost extent we can. But we do not know beforehand how far we may succeed. There is no prescribed bar, so far as appears, beyond which we cannot go. Thus we aim at nothing less than bringing all wills of men and all institutions on earth into conformity with the Will of God, that is, at bringing about a state of things which might be described as a kingdom of God. So long as there is any removable evil, we have to go on striving for its removal. The question then whether, as a matter of fact, future generations of Christians will ever succeed in bringing about such a state of things, is not of practical importance. We are bound in any case to do all we can in our own day to influence the wills and actions of men and modify the institutions of the world in such a way that the world, when we leave it, may have made an advance, however small, towards that goal.

But even if the earthly kingdom is established, not by any sudden appearance of Christ in power to men living on earth, but by a gradual process of human endeavour, it will correspond with the early Christian expectation, if we suppose that, at all events, when the earthly kingdom is established such appearances of Christ should be common. To say that such a supposition is fantastic is obviously illogical, if you believe that the appearances of Christ to His disciples after the Resurrection spoken of in the New Testament were manifestations of a real active Person. People often shrink from the logical consequences of their admissions. Anyone who admits that those alleged appearances of the Risen Christ were real has admitted the possibility in principle of other more general manifestations in overwhelming power and glory. Believers in the appearances of Christ after the Resurrection cannot get away from that implication, even if they have a vein of Rationalism which would make them like to do so.

As commonly manifesting Himself in glory and power to men on earth and conversing with them, Jesus would then be present upon earth even more effectually than in " the days of His flesh." Jesus would indeed have " returned." According to the accounts of the appearances after the Resurrection current in the early Church and preserved in the New Testament, Jesus in all these appearances wore the human form His disciples had known before the Crucifixion, yet changed in some way which prevented them sometimes from immediately recognizing Him.[1] Of course we are not obliged to suppose that in the unseen world the "body" of the Risen Lord has a form with hands and feet and other members adapted to life on this material globe; it may have been only for the purpose of conversing with men still in their earthly bodies that He manifested Himself in a form like theirs, in that form which they had known. The accounts say that He even showed the marks in His body of the nails and the spear. That might have been simply part of the manifestation to those who had witnessed the Crucifixion, to prove that He was the same Person. Charles Wesley's hymn indeed says, of Christ in heaven,

> Those dear tokens of His passion
> Still His dazzling body wears,
> Cause of endless exultation
> To His ransomed worshippers.
> With what rapture
> Gaze we on those glorious scars!

But I doubt whether in our present state we can imagine at all the mode in which Christ presents Himself to the "company of heaven."

There is something more I think we can say. If in some future state of men on earth, manifestations of Jesus in human form will be common, it is consonant to suppose that there will be manifestations, not of Jesus only, but of other persons who have passed through death into the unseen. That, too, would

[1] Luke xxiv. 16; John xxi. 4.

correspond with early Christian anticipations. Jesus will return " with His saints " and will reign " with His saints." The account of the events following the Crucifixion given in St. Matthew affirms that such manifestations in bodily form of a number of the holy men long dead did occur during the days following the Resurrection of Jesus, beside the manifestations of Jesus Himself.[1] No doubt many people will say that such a statement, found only in our First Gospel, which was compiled probably in North Syria in the latter part of the first century, is just part of the legendary material which had grown up there round the remembered events of the life and death of Jesus. It may be so; but, if so, the legend may reflect a true intuition that a re-entry of Jesus from the unseen world into this world would not be confined to Jesus only.

Thus we are presented in imagination with a state of human life on this planet in which it would be an everyday experience to see in bodily form those who had lived on earth in earlier days and had passed through death, to see them and converse with them. If so, they would once more constitute a single fellowship with those on earth who had not yet died, united in constant mutual communications as satisfying as any that the people still in the earthly body have with each other. The screen, as it were, which now separates the unseen world from this would have become pervious from the other side, and although men still in the flesh might be unable to imagine the conditions of the world beyond death and the life of those who belonged to that world, that world would interpenetrate this one and continual converse between the two worlds would go on. Those, I repeat, who believe that Jesus really manifested Himself to His

[1] Matthew xxvii. 52, 53.

disciples after the Resurrection have admitted something which prevents them from calling with any logical consistency such an intercourse between the two worlds as we have supposed a fantastic idea.

CHAPTER VI

THE FAMILIAR MIRACLE

It is apparently God's general will, this discussion has recognized, that the processes of nature in this spatial world should proceed according to uniform laws which are never relaxed by any "supernatural" modification, and thus many people, who still claim to be Christians and still believe in another world into which men enter at death, deny that there have ever been such interferences with natural processes in this world as would constitute "miracles." This is, of course, quite contrary to the traditional belief of the Christian Church, which has affirmed from the beginning that miracles do at rare moments occur, and has regarded two miracles especially as fundamental for the Christian faith—the Birth of Jesus without a human father and the Resurrection of Jesus in His reanimated body from the tomb. Now we must admit that we do all, even the most whole-hearted believers in recorded miracles, regard the material processes with which we have to do in our own practical life, as following inflexible laws, except in so far as they have been modified by human or animal volition. We do not regard the "miraculous" as anything likely to enter into our own experience; from day to day we act on the supposition that the laws governing material processes are uniform. Few people would claim ever to have witnessed a miracle. And those who are adverse to admitting any miraculous element in religious belief may ask of what practical consequence a belief in miracles can be, if miracles cannot enter into our own experience. Suppose we could ourselves expect to walk on the water or see someone whose help we needed come to us walking on the water, then it might be important to believe that Christ had once walked upon the water nineteen hundred years ago; but if that is not something which we can ever regard as a possibility in our own range, it cannot be of much value to us to think that it happened, as an isolated event, once in a remote past.

The discussion in this book has all along avoided building upon a belief in the miraculous, it has not called in question the view that the processes of nature are iron processes to which human life on this planet must be always subject. And I do not myself see that genuine Christian faith absolutely requires a belief in the miraculous, that it is impossible without it.

It does require belief in another world, a field of reality beyond the life of man in his present material body, an eternal world in which persons continue after bodily death. The laws and possibilities of that world must be quite different from the laws and possibilities of this one. But it does not seem to me essential to believe that such interference from that world in the processes of this world as are involved in the miracles of the traditional Christian story occur, or have occurred.

With regard to the Virgin Birth, it is, I should allow, essential to the Christian faith to believe that Jesus was personally identical with God in a way in which no other man ever was or ever can be, a difference not of degree only, but of kind. If the Christian faith had been that He was a being half-God and half-man, it would have been consonant to believe that only one of His parents was human. But the Christian faith is that, while He was God, He was also perfect Man, and there would therefore seem no essential incompatibility between His deity and His having, as other men, two human parents. Belief in the Virgin Birth would then rest simply upon the authority of the Church when it ordained a certain form of words in the Creeds and declared the writings collected in the New Testament to be infallible. How far the authority of the Church does extend to the establishment of facts in past history is, of course, a question which has opened vast volumes of controversy.

With regard to Christ's Resurrection you still have what is essential, if you believe that His appearances to His disciples were the manifestation of a real Person who had passed beyond death into a life of infinitely increased activity, even if you do not believe that the material body in which He was crucified was reanimated. If the world into which He had passed has different laws and possibilities from this one, it may be described, from the point of view of this world as a wonder-world, and the manifestations of the Risen Christ would then be a disclosure of the wonder-world to persons still living under the processes of this world, but such a disclosure in the minds and sense-experience of those persons need not imply any interference with the processes of this world. The appearances of Christ would then, while they were disclosures of the supernatural, hardly constitute "miracles."[1]

If, then, anyone says "I cannot believe that there is ever any such supernatural interference with the laws of the material world as constitutes a miracle: is

[1] It has been often pointed out that in the earliest account of the Resurrection appearances which we have (1 Corinthians xv. 3-8) there is no mention of the Empty Tomb or of the appearances to the women. St. Paul, however, does mention the burying of the Body, and this may imply that his readers would know the

therefore for me the Christian faith absolutely precluded?" I personally should answer, "No: you can still believe in the reality of the other world and the continued spiritual activity of Jesus in this world, even if you do not think that this activity involves any interference with the processes of matter." On the other hand, the assertion that miracles never occur, appears to me ill-founded. The foundation for it is that the processes of matter, so far as experience goes, follow fixed laws from which there is no deviation: if once there were a possibility of these processes being interfered with by the powers of another world, it is said, all Science would become insecure. But it is not true that all the processes which we observe in this world follow only rigid material laws: many of them are interfered with continually by human and animal volition. If such interference makes Science insecure, Science must be pretty insecure already. Science cannot even pretend to reduce the acts of human and animal volition to laws enabling it to predict, except very conjecturally, what the acts are going to be. Of course, many people who want Natural Science to rule everything, do not like this irregular exception. They therefore deny that it is really an exception. It only seems an exception, we are told, because our knowledge is not yet advanced enough to determine the laws of human and animal behaviour as perfectly as we do those of electricity or dynamics. But this is merely an assertion which cannot possibly be proved, and which contradicts the testimony of the human spirit.

The movement of an organic body by its desire of

story of the Empty Tomb. An argument of some force in support of the story is that if the chief priests had been able to produce the Body when a community hostile to them arose in Jerusalem, declaring that Jesus had risen from the dead, they would presumably have done so.

achieving something is different in kind from the movement of a mass of matter by a push from behind. This is recognized by a present-day thinker such as Nicolai Hartmann, even though his theory of the world is atheistic.[1] And the movement of matter by non-material things such as desires, values, fears, is, so far as we know, found on this planet alone in the whole spatial universe. On most of the other globes in space of which Science can speak, it seems definitely impossible that anything like animal life can exist: in none is there any ground for supposing that it does exist. Perhaps nowhere else, could we travel through the whole spatial universe, should we see lumps of matter moving about in the odd way that living bodies do on this earth: we should see only movements of matter without motive, like avalanches and glaciers, and the fall of rocks. One may notice that Modernist theologians who dislike the miraculous generally oppose strongly the idea that life is confined to this planet because they instinctively feel that, if that is so, we are really confronted with the miraculous. But it is only because the idea gives them an uncomfortable feeling, not because there is the faintest scientific ground for rejecting it, that they oppose it. If I rise from my chair, this lump of matter

[1] "Just because it [purposive activity] is different in kind it holds a commanding position. Within the range of its dominion it is, among all the constituents of the universe, the one which gives its ultimate character to the whole. The superiority which it confers upon man in the world does not consist in its exercising the greatest determining force: on the contrary, because of its cosmic smallness and dependence, it is immeasurably weaker than the causal nexus which governs everything all along the line—an infinitesimal drop of real purposive activity in the ocean of essentially purposeless causality (ein verschwindender Tropfen realer Zwecktätigkeit im Meere der ontologisch zweckindifferenten Kausalität). But it sees, foresees, foredetermines; and thereby makes the blind process of events serve its ends."—*Ethik*, p. 188 (in the German edition of 1935).

moving in this way is just as miraculous according to the laws which seem to prevail everywhere else in the universe, as if I rose into the air against gravity. No miracle alleged in religious history is more of a strange exception to the ordinary processes of life on earth than the ordinary processes of life on earth are a strange exception to what goes on throughout the rest of stellar space. If any rational spirit, without foreknowledge, could have surveyed the movements of the matter distributed on the globes through space, some millions of years ago, before the appearance of life on this one infinitesimal planet, he could not have predicted that such a thing as life would ever be, or that matter would ever move in the odd way it does in a living body.

Inasmuch as desires and values and fears, pleasure and pain and memory and thought, belong to a field of reality different from the matter of the spatial world, we may say that that field of reality is, in contrast with the law of the spatial world, a wonder-world. And in the movement of living bodies there *is* an interference by powers of that wonder-world in the material processes of this world. It does not seem miraculous to us because to us who have lived all our lives on this planet the movement of living bodies is something familiar. But if we think of that spirit whom we imagined to survey the spatial universe suddenly seeing on one small globe a lump of matter without any propulsion from without set itself in motion, brandish its extremities, and so move itself from one place to another, he would certainly note it as a very startling interference with processes of this world by the powers of the wonder-world.

Such interference does not seem miraculous to the denizens of the planet because they are familiar with it. And so far as ordinary experience goes, the interferences are confined within a certain range. The only matter moved directly by non-material things, by desires, thoughts, and so on, is the matter constituting the body of the person to whom the desires and thoughts belong. Even within this range we are confronted with an inexplicable fact. Some people, as was said just now, try to make out that the matter is not really moved by the non-material things, but follows its own material laws, and that the non-material things are merely accompaniments which have no share in determining the process (*epiphenomena*). One absurd conclusion to which this theory would logically lead is that, suppose consciousness had never emerged to accompany the material processes of living bodies, the movements of tongue and lips which men make in talking would have gone on just as they have done till to-day, although there would have been no more thought behind them than behind the clatter of a windmill. But when people claim that in stating this theory they are talking in the name of "Science," that is mere bluff, which ought not to impress us. It is simply not true that the theory is held by all men of science of the highest authority. A friend of mine who was interested in some cases of automatic writing which appeared to be communications from some person in the unseen world talked about it to one of our greatest living authorities on Physiology, and said: "I suppose from your point of view, as a man of science, it is inexplicable that a hand could be made to move by a mind other than the writer's?" The great physiologist replied: "Not a bit more inexplicable than that a thought in your mind should make your hand write: that is as much an enigma to Science to-day as it ever was."

But if this movement of matter by mind is something inexplicable—a miracle from the point of view of a spirit who surveyed the rest of the spatial universe, we can have no *a priori* reason for saying that the movement of matter by mind never occurs except in the case of men's or animals' minds moving their own bodies. Disbelief in any movement of matter by mind other than the movement by men and animals of their own bodies is not based on any philosophical principle, but simply on a certain range of experience. Exceptional cases are alleged to occur even to-day of material masses being moved by psychic power. I have known perfectly sane, well-educated people who told me that they had actually witnessed with their own eyes tables being moved without contact. I don't think that any such case has been completely proved: the possibilities of self-deception and tricks of memory are great. On the other hand, when the ordinary movement of a living body is so inexplicable, so really a miracle in respect of what obtains in the universe elsewhere than on this earth, it seems to me quite unreasonable to pronounce it impossible that in certain peculiar cases the movement of matter by mind may go further. If I saw a table move across the room after some person who rose to go away, as a friend of mine assures me she once saw in her own home, and if the circumstances excluded the hypothesis of trickery, it would not really be a bit more miraculous than the first movements of living bodies on one particular globe among the millions in space. Suppose it is true that such rare cases occur, then we should expect the evidence for them to be very much what it is to-day for "psychic phenomena"—the witness of individuals here and there which could not quite amount to conclusive proof. And there is one other thing we should expect. If one such case were really witnessed—say a case of levitation, a body raised into the air, to which there is a certain amount of testimony throughout the ages—then the idea of it would be suggested to a large number of people beside the person or persons who witnessed the phenomenon, and the real case would generate a whole number of imaginary and fictitious cases. Even if levitation sometimes occurs it is likely that a great majority of the alleged cases are imaginary or fictitious. The existence of this cloud of false stories does not prove that there was not a real case, or several real cases, which gave rise to them. It would be analogous to what happens in the case of atrocity stories. Whenever atrocities are perpetrated by any set of people in any part of the earth, it is likely that the true stories will give rise to a cloud of false ones. This leads some people to refuse credit to any atrocity stories—or any charges of committing such atrocities made against the people of whom they desire to think well—Nazis or Bolsheviks or Turks or Japanese. Such uncritical scepticism is just as likely to mislead as uncritical credulity.

But whether we think or not that movements of matter by mind other than the everyday movements of living bodies have ever occurred, when we have to-day in the movement of living bodies an inexplicable movement of matter by mind, there is plainly a possibility that the future may bring a much extended movement of matter in ways we cannot forecast now. The early Christian expectation that a kingdom of God will come on earth in which the material conditions will be largely changed by an extension in this world of the operations of the wonder-world beyond, cannot be considered in itself absurd. The surveyor of the inanimate universe before the beginning of life on earth, if he saw the first stirrings of matter by sentient life in the trilobites of the Silurian oceans, could not have forecast what manifestations this strange new principle working in the material world would come to later on in the higher animals and in man. It may be that when we look at these manifestations in animals and men to-day and forecast the future, we are in the position of that imagined surveyor looking at the trilobites, as unable as he would have been to divine what extensions the operation of mind in the material world will have from fresh beginnings in the age to come.

CHAPTER VII

LEFT-WING CHRISTIANITY

This brings us to the consideration of a movement which has gained a certain following in recent years, mainly, I think, among the younger members of the student community. It is commonly referred to as "Left-wing Christianity" or "Christianity of the Left." Its main contention is that the troubles of the world would be largely cured if a Communist order were substituted for the present Capitalist order, and since it also believes that it is the duty of Christians to bring about the best condition of things possible on this earth, it insists that Christians ought to direct their activities to bringing in Communism. So far there would be little to distinguish the "Left-wing Christianity" of our day from the Christian Socialism which has existed from the days of Kingsley and Maurice, and which has been represented by Christian leaders of as Catholic a faith and as fine and lovable a spirit as Charles Gore. That it is the duty of Christians to bring about the best condition of things on this earth which they have it in their power to bring about no Christian, I imagine, would question, though the majority of Christians do not think that things would be made better by their trying to bring about a Socialist or Communist order. But even those Christians who think Christian Socialists wrong in setting their hopes on Socialism should admit that, if any Christians really believe that the establishment of Socialism would bring about a better world, they are bound to strive for it; disagreement on the question whether, as a matter of fact, a Socialist world would be a better world or not need not imply any disagreement on the substance of the Christian faith. It is true that Christian Socialists, from Kingsley and Maurice onwards, have thought that Christians, while looking for a better world beyond earthly life, have not been interested enough in making this world better, have acquiesced too easily in the evils attaching to our present Capitalist system. But Christian Socialists of the past, Christian Socialists of the school of Charles Gore (and I think I might add of Professor Raven, their historian) have never held that the main task of the Christian Church was to improve social conditions on this earth. They have been quite clear that the Church's main interest was *jenseits*, "on the other side beyond," as the Germans say, or, as we generally say, "other-worldly," that its main task was to bring men in this life to fit themselves for the life of heaven. Only they have insisted that the effort to improve things here is an essential part of that main task, that existing social evils are among the great hindrances to men being fitted for the life which, beginning here, reaches into eternity beyond, that neglect to combat these evils, to supply, so far as it is within the power of Christians, the earthly needs of men, often makes the proclamation of the Christian Good News a sound on the air without effect. Christ, whose spirit is represented in the Fourth Gospel by the words "Work not for the meat which perisheth, but for the meat which abideth unto eternal life," was also concerned that the multitude should be fed with the meat which perisheth, lest they should faint by the way.

This has been the doctrine of the Christian Socialists of the Kingsley-Maurice tradition till to-day. What differentiates the new "Christianity of the Left" is its insistence that the establishment of a Communist order is no longer to be regarded as a task subservient to the Church's main task of forming a community for the life beyond: interest in the life beyond is actually a rival to interest in making this world better; and it would have the Church's interest shifted, mainly or entirely, to this world. Christianity should be a *dies-seits* religion, a this-worldly religion. The extreme representatives of this "Christianity of the Left," such as Professor John Macmurray, appear even to deny that there *is* any life beyond; all hopes and beliefs that go beyond man's life of some few score years are illusion. When bodily death comes we cease to exist. Jesus, we are, I suppose, to understand according to this queer version of Christianity, ceased to exist nineteen hundred years ago. This extreme view is the only logical one if the Church has no task beyond that of improving conditions on earth. To profess to believe in an eternal life beyond and to say that it is less important than the brief life on earth is manifestly absurd. Those "Christians of the Left" who want Christianity to be essentially a this-world religion and shrink from going the length of Professor Macmurray, hold a miserable half-way position.

Of course it is nothing new to maintain that the life we live on earth is all the existence we have, and that all ideas of a future life or a life of spirits in the Unseen are illusions. That has been asserted by secularists and materialists in opposition to the Christian faith, and to all other non-Christian religions, ever since there has been any Christian Church. Through nineteen centuries those who defended the Christian faith have given their grounds for believing that the unseen spiritual world is real and that personal existence goes on beyond death. What is odd in "Left-wing Christianity" is that, while it agrees with materialism in denying beliefs for which everything called Christianity has always stood, it seeks to combine the denial with an assumption of the Christian name. Why, it might be asked, should those who dislike so much the beliefs of Christians wish to be considered Christians themselves? To the plain materialist or secularist who frankly calls Christianity false it must seem an absurd freak. It is not to be thought that they assume a Christian guise in order to destroy within the Christian camp the beliefs of Christians, just as the soldiers of an army at war are sometimes dropped, we are told, by parachutes behind the enemy's lines in the enemy's uniform. I think the reason probably is that for them themselves too certain associations of feeling cling to the Christian tradition, so that it gives them a satisfaction to regard themselves as Christians even when they attack Christian beliefs. This is especially so if they can find among the sayings of Jesus some upon which a meaning may be put confirmatory of their own philosophy, and so gain for it the persuasiveness belonging to that supreme Name.

Nothing is easier than to make any Jesus you like out of the documents. You have only to leave out whatever does not fit in with your purpose and fill in the gaps with your own imagination. The French Communist writer, Henri Barbusse, wrote a book to show that Jesus was really a revolutionary atheist. Quite simple to do, though it means leaving out a good deal! "Left-wing Christianity" does not, of course, mind coming into conflict with traditional orthodoxy, but neither does it mind apparently coming into conflict with the results of modern critical scholarship. It is as ready to pick the sayings of Jesus it wants out of the Fourth Gospel as out of the Synoptists, though nothing could be more utterly destructive of its this-worldly view than the Fourth Gospel, taken as a whole.

Similarly, it likes to claim that it is reproducing the outlook of the primitive Christian community, because in that community the expectation of a kingdom of God on earth was widespread. It is quite reckless in its misrepresentation of historical fact. A mere readjustment of social relations by human effort on an earth whose physical conditions remain what they are now is something very different from the primitive Christian hope. For those early disciples the kingdom they expected on earth was only a temporary prelude to the eternal state in which, after the Resurrection, the redeemed would be united. Thus it is quite misleading to say, as Mr. Joseph Needham does:[1] "The Christians of the primitive church put their kingdom on the earth." Nor was the earthly kingdom to be established by human effort, but by an irruption of supernatural power. And its conditions would be miraculous. In a passage quoted from Papias, Mr. Needham sees an anticipation of an abundance of natural wealth latent in the world's productive forces. The materialist realism of the description is welcome from the point of view of a this-worldly religion. When Mr. Needham speaks of the saying quoted as one "believed to be an authentic saying of Christ Himself," he must mean that it was believed by Papias or Irenaeus to be that, though an uninformed reader might understand him to mean that it was believed to-day to be an authentic saying of Christ. We know to-day that it was really

[1] *Christianity and the Social Revolution*, p. 427. (Gollancz, 1935.)

drawn from a Jewish apocalypse.[1] Not only would conditions on earth be miraculously transformed but it was expected, as we have seen, that Jesus Himself would be visibly present in the body of His Resurrection and that others who had died would be raised again to reign with Him—this world interpenetrated by the wonder-world indeed!

We find in the contemporary Judaism an expectation analogous to the Christian expectation of a millennium coming before the eternal state. Later on the Rabbis definitely distinguished " the days of the Messiah " from " the World to Come." The duration of the reign of the Messiah is variously given; in iv Ezra it is 400 years; in Rabbinic literature it varies from 40 years to 7,000 years; one authority gives 365,000 years.[2] One difference between the Christian and the Rabbinic view is to be noted: according to the Rabbis the habitation of the blessed in " the World to Come " is still this earth, though this earth changed into a wonder-world, enduring for all eternity, whose inhabitants have all been raised from the dead and can die no more. And this view may seem more logical than the view which came to prevail in

[1] Either 2 Baruch xxix. 5 (R. H. Charles, *Apocrypha and Pseudepigrapha of the Old Testament*, vol. ii, p. 497) or some common source further back.

[2] The material is all put together in Strack and Billerbeck, *Kommentar zum Neuen Testament*, vol. iv (the fifth volume as bound), Excursus 29. Professor H. Loewe, Reader in Rabbinics in Cambridge, tells me that he considers Strack and Billerbeck to go too far in making a firm dogmatic system out of the multifarious utterances dispersed through Rabbinic literature; and this was the view also taken by his predecessor, the late Professor Israel Abrahams. Nevertheless, the distinction between the temporary reign of the Messiah and the eternal " World to Come," however the details were drawn, was general. The Resurrection was usually expected to come *after* the reign of the Messiah, as it does in the Christian Book of Revelation, though the Christians who have undergone martyrdom are there raised at the coming of the Messiah to reign with Him in His earthly kingdom.

the Christian Church, when it was laid down that at the Resurrection everyone would have a body similar in form to his earthly body, with all the members which had served for life on earth complete, whereas the sphere in which these re-embodied persons would dwell would be an unearthly spiritual one. The Rabbis may reasonably have held that if a man after the Resurrection was to have his two feet as before, his dwelling should be where there was earthly ground for him to walk on. Most modern Christians do not think that the body in which the discarnate spirit is clad has a form like an earthly body, but implies means of self-expression and communication adapted to the wholly different conditions of a world not included in the three-dimensional space we know.

In any case never was a temporary earthly kingdom regarded by primitive Christians as the ultimate fulfilment of their hope: that was always the union of the Divine Community in heaven. "Left-wing Christianity" simply puts an imagination of its own in the place of the real historical early Christianity. The great charge it brings against the hope of life beyond death is that it is "wishful thinking": a future wonder-world is pictured without any basis in facts. Well, there can be wishful thinking in regard to the past, as well as in regard to the future. And there is one obvious difference between them: the anticipation of a future beyond the world, even if it cannot rest upon the facts of this world, cannot at any rate come into conflict with facts, because future facts do not yet exist, whereas wishful thinking about the past *is* liable to come into conflict with the facts, as ascertained by competent inquiry.

This apparent indifference to truth is an unhappy consequence, I think, of an excessive insistence upon the subordination of knowledge to action characteristic of Left-wing philosophy. No doubt it is right in closely associating intellectual apprehension with practical activity, but if you get into the way of treating knowledge apart from action as marking an idle contemplative attitude to the universe, very inferior in worth, you slip easily into the way of asserting anything to be true which is convenient for your purposes. It is common to point to something admirable in the scientific temper which, by a kind of ascetic renunciation, tries to arrive at the truth purely on the evidence of facts already ascertained, without allowing any desires for practical advantage to shape the conclusion. It is true that the ideal man of science is an abstraction, and that no human being in actual life could have this pure disinterested love of truth as his sole motive. Yet it is very dangerous to disparage the love of truth which sternly shuts out considerations of practical advantage, and seeks to determine precisely what the evidence implies, however unwelcome the consequences. Perhaps we may see the consequences of such disparagement in the readiness with which "Left-wing Christianity" constructs the Jesus it wants, the primitive Church it wants, and lightly dismisses whatever in the evidence it finds unserviceable.

"Left-wing Christianity" has a word by which it thinks apparently it can make short work of any opposing view. That word is "dualism." If you say of any belief you don't like, "That is dualism," you refute it without further ado. "Dualism" in the Christian tradition has a condemnatory sound because it has been used to distinguish the Zoroastrian view and the Gnostic view from the Christian view. Zoroastrian doctrine was dualist inasmuch as it put the Evil Power almost on an original level with the Good Power, in the production and governance of the world, whereas for Christians everything that was had been created good by God; spiritual evil was only the rebellion of beings whom God had endowed with the power to choose, and the operation of evil was confined within the limits imposed by God's Will. The Gnostics held that one element in the world, Matter, was essentially evil, whereas Christians held that Matter, like Spirit, had been created good by God though it could be used by spirits for evil ends. Thus the Church has strongly repudiated the Zoroastrian and Gnostic view, so far as these differed from the Christian view, as dualist. But as " Left-wing Christianity " uses the term " dualist " it can be applied to any view which supposes any contrast of quality or worth between one element of the world and another, one part of the universe and another. To believe, for instance, that there is a real world of spirits beside the world we know by our bodily senses, that human life has extension beyond bodily death, certainly implies a contrast between this world and the other world, this life and the other life, but it is not " dualist " in any other sense, because it regards all worlds and all conscious beings there may be as included in God's universe. Of course, the Christian faith implies that there are at least two worlds. But if you say " There cannot be another world beside this because then the universe would include two different fields of reality," it is an absurd begging of the question: " There cannot be two worlds because then there would be two worlds." Why should there not be two worlds, or any number of worlds?

Christianity repudiated Zoroastrian dualism, but one has to recognize how near in many respects Christianity, and the later Judaism out of which it arose, came to it. The Old Testament, as was said, has a dim, dark conception of the existence of men in the world of the dead, but when Jesus was on earth the only people among the Jews who held out stoutly against "dualism" were the Sadducean priestly aristocracy—the people who were the prime movers in getting Jesus put to death. In the Old Testament, except in one late passage,[1] there is no appearance of Satan as the Evil One; Satan in Job and in Zechariah is shown as an adversary of men, but not yet as an adversary of God. By the time that Jesus was born, Satan had become an overshadowing figure in Jewish belief analogous to Ahriman in Zoroastrianism. True, Satan was less dualist than Ahriman inasmuch as he was thought of as having been originally created good by God, and as controlled all through by God; but it has to be remembered that in Zoroastrianism, too, Ahriman was inferior in power to Ormuzd and destined to be ultimately overcome and abolished. Satan, like Ahriman, was the head of a whole kingdom of innumerable evil spirits, continually interfering in the life of men and the processes of nature. Jesus affirmed this view of an organized kingdom of evil opposed to the kingdom of God to be true. It is hardly possible to have anything more "dualist," according to the use of the term by "Left-wing Christianity," than the words of Jesus about the kingdom of Satan which cannot be divided against itself, since, if it were so disorganized, it could not stand. No discourse of Jesus is better authenticated; it is found in all three Synoptists, and was apparently included in Q as well as in St. Mark.[2] If we go by the discourses attributed to Jesus in the Fourth Gospel, the dualism seems almost pushed to the length of Zoroastrianism, "Ye are of your father the devil. . . . He was a murderer *from the beginning*, and stood not

[1] 1 Chronicles xxi. 1.
[2] Matthew xii. 25-9; Mark iii. 23-7; Luke xi. 17-21.

in the truth, because there is no truth in him."[1] "When he speaketh a lie, he speaketh of his own, for he is a liar and the father thereof."[2]

Christianity repudiated Gnostic dualism, which made Matter essentially evil and believed in an original difference of nature between "fleshly" men and "spiritual" men. But Christianity pushed far the opposition between "flesh" and "spirit," as anyone using a concordance of the New Testament may see, and drew a sharp distinction between "the children of God" and "the children of the Devil."[3] "Dualism" is deep in the Lord's Prayer, with its contrast of heaven and earth and its petition "Deliver us from the Evil One."

If you make insistence upon the contrast and opposition between any two constituents of the universe—between spirit and matter, between good and evil—the ground for a charge of "dualism," you can have no difficulty in convicting any conceivable view of the universe, which does not, like Vedantic Monism, resolve all differences into an underlying One without distinctions, of being dualistic, since all discourse turns upon some sort of differences and contrasts presented by things. In the Old Testament itself some contrasts are insisted upon—"Woe unto them that call evil good, and good evil; that put darkness for light, and light for darkness; that put bitter for sweet and sweet for bitter."[4] If, on the other hand, when you accuse the exponents of Christian doctrines which you happen to dislike of "dualism," you mean that they suppose some part of the universe not to have been created by God or to be beyond His

[1] In Zoroastrianism the Evil One is essentially "the Lie (Druj)": J. H. Moulton, *Early Zoroastrianism*, p. 49.

[2] John viii. 44, 45.

[3] 1 John iii. 10.

[4] Isaiah v. 20.

power to control, then your accusation is false.

The root-fallacy in the "Left-wing Christianity" which denies the existence of any field of reality beyond that of three-dimensional space, is the supposition that belief in a future life and belief in the value of this life are rivals; if you believe in another life beside this one, then this life, it supposes, is necessarily reduced to a mere shadow and unreal show. Nothing could be more absurd. We have only to look at the long tale of those who have toiled most strenuously in making this world in some respect or other a better world, to see how many of them have been Christians whose hope was anchored in the beyond—Howard and Elizabeth Fry, who first fought the horrors of the existing prison-system, Wilberforce and his associates, who carried on the long campaign against slavery, Shaftesbury, who took the lead in getting child-labour in factories abolished. Who to-day bring medical help to thousands of primitive men in far-off regions of the earth, where diseases have been ravaging and torturing human bodies unchecked? Christian missionaries. No doubt very many Christians, who have professed to believe in a future life, have been remiss in efforts to improve conditions on earth, but in most cases that has not been because their imagination of another world was so vivid that their interest was drawn away from this world, but because their religion as a whole was too conventional and humdrum; a more vivid apprehension of a life beyond in which their life here would be laid bare before the judgment seat of Christ would have made them more, not less, energetic in the service of men on earth. If "Left-wing Christians" accuse those who hold fast the other-worldly hope of being remiss in their efforts to make this a better world, it is generally not because they have really been remiss, but because, while they have tried to make it a better world in all sorts of other ways, they have not concentrated their efforts on what seems to " Left-wing Christians " the one thing that matters—bringing in a Communist order. It is true that Christians in general have not; but that, in the case of many ardent Christians, is not because they were insufficiently interested in making this world better, but because they did not believe that the world would be better by being made Communist. And it is no doubt true that Christians in the past have acquiesced too easily in some evils which attached to the existing social and economic order, in the belief that they were inevitable, when a more radical understanding of their causes would have shown that they might be remedied or mitigated. It is also true, in one sense, that belief in another world diminishes the importance of this one. It makes it less important for each individual what *happens to him* here; the pains, the troubles, the privations, the disappointments that befall him he can bear as belonging to a state of things soon to pass away: life, in that sense, has been truly called a dream. But it makes it enormously more important for each individual what he *does* here; eternal issues hang upon that; the character he forms here by the way he deals in action with the material of this world will not pass away. George Tyrrell in that poignant book of his published after his death, *Christianity at the Cross Roads*, maintained that it was precisely Christians who could throw themselves whole-heartedly into fighting the evils of the present state of things, even when such efforts seemed destined to fail, as far as this world went, because they would be training spirits for the life to come.

There may, however, be many who would call

themselves " Left-wing Christians " but who maintain the Christian hope of a life to come with as strong conviction as any Christians have done: only they hold, like the Christian Socialists of an earlier generation, that, while the main task of the Church is to fit men for the life of heaven, it is the duty of Christians to work for a Communist order on earth as the best for men in this life. If so, what has been said in criticism of " Left-wing Christianity " does not touch their position, and they are nearer to their non-Communist fellow-Christians than to the " Left-wing Christians " of whom we have been speaking. They agree with their non-Communist fellow-Christians regarding the importance of the life to come, but disagree with them regarding the best social arrangement in this world, whereas they agree with Professor Macmurray and Mr. Needham only regarding the best social arrangements in this world, but disagree with them regarding the importance of the life to come.

Would a Communistic state of things be the best for the world? Well, that opens immense questions which it would be absurd to try to go into in a part of a chapter of this little book. But there are certain things which may strike anyone, to begin with, who considers attentively the world round him to-day. It cannot be denied that in the " Capitalist " *régime*, as we see it in Western Europe and in America, there are enormous evils—the poverty, the bad housing which, in spite of very great improvements in the last seventy years still mars so many human lives, the uncertainty of employment, unemployment, the contrast with this of a certain number of people who possess riches which they use in self-indulgence, class-distinctions insisted upon in a way to debar human fellowship, and—what perhaps is felt by some of the less fortunate more keenly than material discomforts

—the lack of opportunity for mental and spiritual development.

So long as these things are there, it would plainly be wrong for Christians to acquiesce in the world as it is. If we feel ourselves too inexpert to say precisely what change of institutions would make the world better, we can at any rate go on declaring that until the experts have found the remedy for these things we can never be content.

I do not see how it can be denied that there is a sense in which all Christians ought to be Communists—in spirit, and action. The community of disciples at Jerusalem shown in the first chapters of Acts presents a type of Communism which German writers call "Love Communism." There was no compulsion on the richer members of the community to part with their possessions,[1] but in the general atmosphere of fraternal love pervading the community the richer members did, as a matter of fact, sell much of their property and throw the proceeds into the common fund for the benefit of the poor. "Not one of them said that aught of the things which he possessed was his own; but they had all things common."[2] The phrase "said that none of the things which he possessed was his own" suggests that the people in question did not necessarily cease to be the owners of this or the other piece of property, but that they did not regard it as their own in a selfish way, that they were ready, if occasion required, to let others share in its enjoyment.

Suppose all men were ideal Christians, they would all be perfectly unselfish and we should then have something of the same state of things within each man's circle of neighbours. It would not matter much how large or small an amount of property any

[1] Acts v. 4. [2] Acts iv. 32.

man possessed, because he would hold and use his property for the common good. Any social order now established, whether Capitalist or Communist, is an organization of men who are largely selfish, and whatever the organization may be, the result cannot be wholly satisfactory. You cannot, the proverb says, make a silk purse out of a sow's ear. A Communist order established as a compulsive system would not mean the Love Communism of the primitive Church, but an order in which no one was allowed to possess property of a certain kind or beyond a certain amount. Compulsion would be exercised by the community through that particular executive body which had the direction of things. It would not be left to individuals to produce goods, as they chose, but all that the community required—food, clothing and everything else—would be produced by labour organized under the central directing body. If the communal principle was "To each according to his needs, from each according to his ability," it would be for certain officials appointed with definite functions to determine what each man's needs were and see that the distribution was properly carried out, and for other officials to bring compulsion to bear on those who would not contribute according to their ability. Since men and women who composed such a community would be ordinary specimens of human nature, they would be in streaks selfish and unselfish. Certainly there might be Communist societies in which there was a high level of unselfish devotion, but there would always be a liability for the persons doing a particular kind of work or exercising administrative functions to be slack or dishonest or grasping, and it would be quite possible for a Communist organization to show very poor results because in that particular community the level of unselfish devotion was low; it would be possible for the directing elements to be brutally tyrannical.

If, therefore, many Christians do not think that the attempt to establish a Communist order would make a better world, they would not deny that, supposing you could have a company of angels to determine exactly what each man's needs were and compel him to contribute according to his abilities, you might have a much better state of things than the present. What they are doubtful about is how a system which could only work satisfactorily, if a very high level of unselfish devotion were general among manual craftsmen and directing officials, would work out, if you established it in a society of largely selfish men. It may be said that such a system, even with the run of men largely selfish, would at any rate secure "equality" by preventing anyone from increasing his possessions, and would prevent one set of people from being "superior" to another set. But both "equality" and "superiority" can mean very different things. In England, to-day, which is not Communist, perfect equality exists in some respects between one person and another—everyone, for instance, has equal rights in going to law or being put on trial—though in other respects, such as the amount of possessions and the power to hire service, there is great inequality. Or in regard to "superiority," any society which implies a diversity of functions, as a Communist society would have to do as much as any other, there are certain functions which necessarily confer a superior prestige or power upon those who exercise them, and that kind of superiority a selfish individual may easily assert in a Communist society in as offensive a way as the superiority of a rich man is sometimes asserted in England. Even in a Capitalist society the superiority which wealth gives may be made to serve unselfish ends: a man whose means enable him to hire labour to do the manual work of his household may himself be doing work of public utility which he could not do if his time had to be given to cooking and sweeping carpets. In a Communist society those doing such work of public utility would presumably be spared the necessity of themselves doing manual work by having workers appointed and paid by the community to do it for them; the result might not be so very different. In both cases particular workers do the same manual work to relieve a person doing useful non-manual work for the community: only in one case the payment comes to the manual workers through officials who judge the non-manual work in question to be valuable, whereas in the other case it comes to them from the person himself who does the valuable work and engages the workers. There are many households in England in which master and servants are friends, and the spirit of that early Love Communism prevails: there is no feeling of grievance on the part of those employed because the functions they exercise are humbler in social estimation than those exercised by the employer, and in such cases there is likely to be more personal fellowships between employer and employed than there would be in a Communist order between the non-manual worker and the persons appointed by the communal authorities to do his domestic work for him.

When I am told that Communism is the way out of our troubles, I cannot help reflecting that what we have here put before us is a contrast drawn between an existing state of things and an imagined state of things. Every existing state of things, human nature being what it is, is bound to have evils attaching to it in practice, whereas, when you draw an imaginary state of things, you can leave all evils out of your picture. The contrast is thus not a fair one. No actualization of Communism can be pointed to which shows a society undoubtedly happier than that in "Capitalist" countries to-day. Russia? Well, the testimonies regarding conditions in Russia are very conflicting. I seem to notice that those who paint them as admirable are usually people who know them only from Bolshevik official statistics (which are alleged on the other side to be utterly misleading)[1] and from occasional visits to Moscow, while those who describe them as quite horrible are usually people who have lived for some considerable time in the country.[2]

Another thing which seems obvious is that while the Capitalist system, as it exists to-day in Western Europe and in America shows the evils just indicated, it does serve the community by supplying some of its

[1] "The reports, accounts and statistics do not reflect the real situation. Every verification or inspection reveals a lie, every analysis uncovers a snare. Comparisons in arbitrary and variable roubles teach nothing. Quantitative progress appears fallacious when one knows the corresponding investments, apart from the waste which must be deducted. Craft production, so important in former times in Russia, reached its lowest point in 1937, and does not figure in those flattering comparisons. Estimates of the national income are so much pure fantasy."—B. Souvarine, *Stalin*, p. 664.

[2] One may refer to two books which seem solid records of fact, *Assignment in Utopia* by Eugene Lyons, and *Stalin* by Boris Souvarine (Secker and Warburg). Of course, eulogists of the present state of things in Russia may refuse to believe the testimony of these writers as they would any other testimony which does not gratify their wishful thinking about Russia. A friend of mine, an expert economist, on whose word I personally rely, who went to Russia an ardent Communist and remained there for a series of years, supports entirely the account of things given by Lyons and Souvarine. If their account is at all true, then the present *régime* in Russia, in claiming to exhibit a new and better civilization, is the most prodigious erection of humbug in human history—"the immense charnel-house of this gigantic prison which with double irony is called 'a Socialist fatherland.'" —Souvarine, *Stalin*, p. 670.

elementary needs. We can imagine a worse state of things, and one has to reckon with the possibility that, if it were disrupted, the subsequent state of things might be a great deal worse. It is dreadful that in Great Britain there should be between one and two million unemployed, but one has to remember on the other side, that there are fifteen million insured wage-earners provided with employment, all by their work supplying the community with things it needs—or thinks it needs, or can be made to think it needs. Take, for instance, the matter of boots. There is a competition between the makers of boots to supply the most satisfactory boots for the lowest price, and for that reason we all of us, including the masses of the poor, can procure as good boots as can be supplied for the price we are able to pay. The motive of the makers of boots is, of course, pecuniary profit, but they stand to gain most by supplying thousands of people with the most satisfactory article for the lowest price. We can imagine a state of things in which it would be difficult for anybody to get a decent pair of boots. Or take again such a vast capitalist enterprise as Woolworth's. It unquestionably enables multitudes of the poor to procure things they want of domestic use at a very low price. In contrast, the Bolshevik system seems to have been very much less successful in supplying the mass of the people with the common goods they need. It would no doubt be wrong to say that no other motive beside that of pecuniary profit could induce the makers of boots or other articles in a Communist society to work as hard to supply the needs of the community, but it would plainly be as well, while you are about destroying the Capitalist system, to make sure that some equally compulsive motive is there ready to take the place of that of pecuniary profit.

Yet again: it is only in the Capitalist democracies

to-day that there is freedom for inquiry and for the public expression of opinion. Even those who admire Russia generally admit that opinion is there shaped by state compulsion and that criticism of the *régime* is confined within very narrow limits. Now it may be regarded as just an old bourgeois-Liberal prepossession to attach great value to freedom for inquiry and the expression of thought, yet to those of us who have that prepossession there are few things so abhorrent as the trussing of man's intellectual faculties and the stereotyping of opinion by the group in power. No doubt when you have a Government unreplaceable by the votes of the governed, it is impossible for unrestrained vituperation of the Government in the press and on the platform to be allowed. A hatred of the Government may be worked up in that way which has no constitutional outlet and so endangers public order. This has been the case, for instance, in India, where the demand for a completely free press could be satisfied only as advance has been made to a state of things in which Governments are replaceable. Yet there has been always an enormously greater freedom for the expression of opinion in India under British rule than there is to-day in Russia or Germany under a native autocracy. I was sent once for a period to an Indian nationalist newspaper, at a time when there were frequent complaints of the press in India being "muzzled." I can only say that, to judge by the continued attacks on the Government in that organ, the muzzle must have been a very wide one. Anybody in Russia or Germany criticizing the Government as Indian nationalist leaders have done for a generation or two past would not have been put in temporary confinement under humane conditions; they would have been killed. So far as I know, no Indian nationalist leader has been executed. It would, I believe, be true to say that, while the autocratic rule of one people by another can never be regarded as satisfactory, whatever special circumstances may justify it as a temporary expedient, the methods used by the British Government in India, compared with those used by any other foreign government known in history, to maintain its authority, appear remarkably mild. It is alleged that in the matter of beating, the police, mainly recruited from sections of the Indian community, have on some occasions been guilty of indefensible excesses. This may, I fear, be true, but, if so, whereas in India you have occasional cases of beating, in Russia or Germany you have, not only beating, but prolonged torture and extensive shooting without trial. Pandit Jawaharlal Nehru, in his interesting and moving autobiography, wishes no doubt to exhibit the foreign rule in the most unfavourable light; yet the fact in itself that such a book is published and circulated without let or hindrance, and sympathetically reviewed in some English papers, the fact that Pandit Nehru is alive at all and at liberty, shows the vast difference between the British Empire and the totalitarian states, in which such a thing, in the case of an opponent of the Government, would be utterly unthinkable. And if this difference exists it is because the Englishmen who take part in the government of India have been educated in an environment in which freedom for inquiry and the expression of opinion is valued. Even suppose a Communist *régime* got rid of many of the ills of the present Capitalist system, it might be thought to do so at too great cost, if it stereotyped opinion and abolished freedom for the utterance of thought.[1] You may be confronted with the old prob-

[1] The expressions "freedom of thought," "free-thinker," are absurd; thought cannot but be free, what can be suppressed is

lem of reconciling "equality" with "liberty."

If there is any substance in these reflections, it may be doubtful whether an attempt to replace the present state of things by a Communist one would lead to any increase of human happiness. Of course this ought not to make us acquiesce in the evils of the present state of things. All Christians who have adequate knowledge of economics, in theory and practice, and are in a position to act in any way upon the course of things, whether as politicians or writers or by informal influence, ought to be constantly wrestling with the problem—as no doubt many of them are. I do not propose to say here anything about promising lines of social reform, firstly because I have *not* the adequate knowledge of economics, and, secondly, because this book is about something else. I may only venture to set down some questions which haunt my mind regarding an effect which Left-wing Christianity may have upon ordinary young men and women in the student stage, a not altogether happy effect.

I think we should all agree so far—that any young man who enters upon life to-day with a serious purpose ought to feel concern for the evils of our present system and think about them. But if he is made to believe that the principal thing in his religion, as a Christian, should be to change radically the economic basis of society, I foresee the likelihood of a certain

the utterance of thought. It is the more absurd when a man to-day who rejects some religious belief claims to be a "free-thinker," because to-day in Britain there is as complete liberty for the utterance of atheistic opinion as for Christian or any other religious belief. There was, no doubt, a time when this was not so, and those who expressed "infidel" opinions were then acting in defiance of constraint exercised by the law or by society. To-day when an atheistic or agnostic claims to be "free" in a peculiar way it is all sham bravery, as if the penalties which atheists long ago had to face were still to be incurred.

misdirection in his life. For he will have around him a large number of duties to those in his immediate environment—his family and friends and business associates and neighbours—which will call every day and immediately for his attention under the existing state of things, whereas the chances of his doing anything to change the basis of society will come rarely, if at all.

Let us suppose, for a moment, that the people are right who want the basis changed to Communism. How are you going to set about it? There are two ways, and two ways only, in which it could come about—one is a violent revolution, in which the existing order was overthrown by an armed rising of the population; the other is by a gradual process of legislative change. The recommendation of the first way is that the desired change would come about quickly. But if a young man is going to work to bring it about in that way, there are some considerations which bear on the enterprise. It being so obvious that a violent revolution would involve bloodshed and suffering on a great scale at the time, and a heritage of hatred afterwards, anyone considering that mode of procedure—we may take it for granted—will already have made up his mind that the achievement of a Communist state is so great a thing that bloodshed and suffering and hatred are all outweighed. But there is another thing to be considered. No violent revolution can be carried through except when the armed forces of the State—soldiers and police—join the insurgents. This was shown in the French Revolution and in the Russian Revolution. It was never more absurd than it is to-day, when Governments in power have such means of destruction at their disposal, to think that any uprising of a casually armed proletariat, any fighting on barricades, can overthrow a Government, so long as the Government's armed forces stick to it. In Britain the likelihood of the Navy, Army and Air Force taking the side of revolutionaries against the constitutionally established Government seems so remote as to be fantastic. Of course, if Britain suffered a shattering defeat in war, so that the food upon which its population depends could not be imported from overseas, anything might happen, but no one to-day can shape his life on the supposition of such an event happening. Short of this happening, it would seem a hopeless enterprise to try to shake the loyalty of the armed forces to the existing Government. And yet, unless anyone thinks he can do something towards effecting this, it is futile for him to make it the object for his life to bring about a violent Communist revolution. Thus any young man who sincerely determines to devote his life to such an end must exert himself, so far as he can within the range of his opportunities—stealthily, of course, so as to elude the vigilance of the police—in trying to instil revolutionary Communism into the individual soldiers, sailors and airmen with whom he comes in contact. I do not think most adherents of "Left-wing Christianity" would like to enter upon such a line of activity; I think, even if they did like it, their opportunities of effecting anything would, in most cases, be *nil*. Then it is obviously better to choose as one's aim in life something more compassable.

It may be objected that even an unarmed proletariat might compel a surrender of the Government by a general strike. This idea was very rife before the experiment of 1926, but since then it has been generally abandoned. It is, I believe, perfectly true that the life of the country would be stopped by a strike of the main body of manual workers in the industries which supply food and other primal necessities to the community, if it could be carried on long enough. But what the experiment of 1926 showed was that at such a conjuncture the British *bourgeoisie* was sufficiently numerous and energetic to take things into its hands. Hundreds of young middle-class Englishmen have interested themselves in some kind of mechanics, fiddling about with motor-cars and engines, and at a pinch are ready enough to take on the work required to maintain for a time the essential services. No doubt they are less efficient than the regular skilled workmen, and the community could not go on permanently without the labour which the strikers have withdrawn. But it could have gone on much longer than the strike lasted in 1926; it is known that large bodies of young men were in training to drive engines and buses, as volunteers, when the strike ended, and it seems likely that in Britain the *bourgeoisie* could always carry on without the manual workers who go on strike longer than the strikers, if they remained passive, could continue to feed themselves. If they do not remain passive but begin to attack the volunteer workers, we have no longer the experiment of subduing *bourgeois* resistance by merely withholding labour, but an appeal to force, and it then becomes just a case of a casually armed proletariat trying to overthrow a fully armed Government.

There remains the other way of bringing about a Communist *régime*—a gradual process of legislative change. Here the essential condition for going forward is the obtaining of a majority of votes in a majority of constituencies in Parliamentary elections for candidates who will vote for Socialist measures. Elections come, as a rule, only every three or four or five years, and suppose those working for the Communist cause have failed at any date to secure a majority of Socialists in the House of Commons, they will have to wait all that time before trying again. If they have secured a majority which will make some small advance in the Communist direction, and continue in successive elections to secure further small advances—if there are none of those swings of the political pendulum which commonly check movement in any one uniform direction—then the sum total of the small advances might in the end bring us to the Communist paradise. But with elections occurring only at intervals of four or five years, the process might well extend beyond the fourscore years allotted to anyone now alive. There does not at present seem any probability of a sudden landslide which would raise the Communist representation in the House from one or two to an absolute majority. At any rate, if anyone is keen to bring about a Communist *régime* by a gradual legislative process his activities will be fruitful simply in so far as he can induce a larger number of people to vote Labour or Communist when the next election time comes. A young man who engages in canvassing, in attending meetings, in distributing literature, may certainly increase the number of those who vote Labour at the next election. Yet the young men who have the opportunity and the ability to increase by their efforts the number of voters for any party to any large extent are few. Some constituencies, like the one in which the writer of this book lives, always return Conservatives by an unassailable majority; in some there is no contest at all. If a young man, living in such a constituency, has been induced to believe that the main thing in a Christian's life should be to break up the present basis of society and replace it by a Communist one, his activities as a Christian will probably be doomed to complete frustration. And all the time, for all of us, there are the people in immediate contact with us toward whom we can act, each common day that passes, while the present order goes on, in a spirit of fellowship and unselfishness—the old Christian virtues which are quite independent of "Left-wing Christianity." There is, I think, a danger that "Left-wing Christianity" may in these cases divert a man, from attending to what he really can do, to Utopian dreaming.

There are unquestionably some men whose abilities and opportunities constitute a call to political work, and if there is some evil requiring a crusade for its suppression, ordinary people in the mass of the population may, within the range of their influence, help to create a public opinion which will, sooner or later, give the crusade success. Two notable instances of such crusades already referred to may encourage the most ordinary people to contribute their own small weight in similar cases to the general push—the crusade against slavery and the crusade against child-labour. But it has to be noted that the objective in these cases was a narrowly limited one. All that was needed to secure triumph for the cause was the passage of an Act, or of a few Acts, through Parliament. After a number of elections the requisite majority in Parliament was secured, and the thing was done. But it is plainly a different business if your objective is the very large and vague one—a break up of the basis of society and its replacement by a new order. The largeness of the objective may dissipate efforts for its attainment, whereas efforts can be concentrated on a more limited and clearly defined one with a much better chance of success. Thus it may be that those who to-day are keen to make a better world would do well, instead of trying to bring in a whole new order at once, to fix upon some particular evil in the present order and concentrate first, as Wilberforce and Shaftesbury did, upon that. It is often said that the legislation of the last fifty years has already, bit by bit, actualized a good deal of the Socialist programme—most notably perhaps in the matter of death duties, housing, Trade Unions, and education. No doubt we are still far from a satisfactory state of things.

CHAPTER VIII

PACIFISM

At the present moment when we speak of the hope to bring in a better world it is not so much social reform within the several national states that we are thinking of as the ordering of international relations. For the moment the horror which is filling our minds is continued war between the national states: so long as that goes on, we see that the hope of internal social reform is impeded or held up altogether. If we are Christians, what ought we to do about it?

The answer is simplest for those who are pacifists. We ought to refuse to take any part in war ourselves, be conscientious objectors, whenever the State brings in conscription, and do our best to persuade other Christians to act in the same way. The weakness of most pacifism is that those who profess it do not fully and resolutely set before themselves the consequences to the world, suppose all Christians refused to fight. They contrast the horror of war with an imagined continuance of the state of things existing before war was begun, and, of course, when set beside war, the continuance of the previous peaceable state of things looks infinitely preferable. In many cases, supposing the evil will was not resisted by force, the previous peaceable state of things would not go on, and the real contrast which is relevant to our decision is that between the horror of war and the horror of what must follow supposing the evil will breaks up the existing state of things and gets its way unchecked. An honest pacifist ought to think out in detail, so far as he can, these consequences. Pacifists seldom do; they generally indulge in an absurd optimism regarding the alternative course to war: they seem to believe that if the aggressor is not checked, he will not be able to effect much anyway, or that if he is spoken nicely to and invited to a conference he will agree to a reasonable compromise.[1] It is possible to face all the consequences likely to follow from the evil will getting its way and still be a pacifist. A Quaker, on his principles, might do so. He may say: "I recognize that all the dreadful consequences you point out are likely to follow, if the evil will is not checked, and I recognize that these dreadful things might be prevented, if my nation engaged in war to check the evil will. But my duty is to obey the command of Christ not to resist the evil will by force; the consequences of my obedience, be they what they may be, are God's concern, not mine. If it is God's will that the evil will should inflict untold miseries on the world in the present age, so be it. In the end, in another world, if not in this one, the victory of good over evil will be

[1] In an early stage of the Italian invasion of Abyssinia a prominent pacifist, Lord Ponsonby, deprecated our doing anything drastic to stop the Italians. He said, addressing the House of Lords (December 19, 1935): "My noble friend who addressed the House last is inclined to think that the Italian Army may succeed in its venture. I have never thought so. If Signor Mussolini had been left at the start, to use a vulgar phrase, to stew in his own juice, he would have found that he had bitten off a great deal more than he could chew. If that is a mixed metaphor, anyhow it is perfectly clear what it means, and it may emphasize my argument outside the walls of this House. It would take this country several years to conquer Abyssinia, and the Italians do not seem to be making any great headway so far. There are stronger things than sanctions, and these are the things that Nature has provided Ethiopia with. Had Signor Mussolini been left alone he would have found that he had taken on a very doubtful task, and very likely he would have been ready to have come to the Council Table."

secured for ever and the sufferings of the faithful, inflicted upon them now by the evil will, will find full compensation. Thus no picture you may set before me of the consequences which will probably follow, if Christians refuse to fight, affects my action at all. I look squarely at the picture, and nevertheless obey Christ."

That is honest pacifism, and against that most of the arguments urged against ordinary pacifism fall dead. Ordinary pacifism shrinks from such a position, and pretends instead that the world will be very much the same as it is now, even if the evil will does get its way unchecked. It proceeds on the silliest of maxims, that "force settles nothing." The only argument which can touch the position of the honest pacifist concerns the question whether, as a matter of fact, Jesus has given a command to His disciples throughout the ages never, in any circumstances, to resist the evil will by force. Quakers, building on a few sentences in His discourses, as reported in the New Testament, which admittedly do, if taken by themselves in isolation, point that way, say that He has; the great majority of Christians throughout the ages have held that when you take the sayings of Jesus in their total context, constituted by the Jewish tradition which was their background, and the particular circumstances which Jesus seems in His several utterances to have had in view, when further you interpret them in the light of a reasonable consideration of the facts of the world and human history as a whole, Jesus has not given any such absolute command. Which view is the true one cannot, I think, be decided by controversial argument. The question has been debated to and fro pretty continuously ever since the outbreak of war in 1914. I remember in those years following 1914 the frequent meetings of different religious groups to discuss and argue about it. I never now see any argument brought forward on either side which has not been advanced a thousand times already and answered a thousand times by the other side. In the end, everyone bases his judgment in the matter upon his total personal reaction to the facts of the world and the religious doctrines in the field, and I doubt whether anybody who has made up his mind one way or the other will now be brought to change his opinion by renewed application to him of any of the old thrashed-out arguments on the opposite side. Personally, I have no great respect for ordinary pacifism, but very great respect for the Quaker position, though I think it mistaken. Having said what I have just now regarding the uselessness of further argument, I will not attempt to justify the view opposed to pacifism by argument here; I should not be able to say anything new.

At least, there is only one argument, occasionally brought forward on the pacifist side, which I might glance at. I have known it brought forward by men rightly held in great respect—the lost beloved Dick Sheppard among them—though how it is possible for anyone who thinks twice to attach the slightest value to it I cannot understand. The argument is that Christians ought not to engage in war because one of the Ten Commandments is "Thou shalt not kill." Consider: there are two different views held of the Old Testament. One is the "Fundamentalist" view that every statement in it is dictated by God and immune from any kind of error. The other is the "Modernist" view which sees in the Old Testament a collection of documents, in many parts legendary and unhistorical, marked throughout by human imagination and human fallibility, but yet embodying a history in which men are seen led to truer and fuller apprehension of God by an operation in their minds of the Divine Spirit. If you take the Fundamentalist view then the command "Thou shalt not kill" was really written by the finger of God upon tables of stone; but then also all the rest of the Old Testament which forms the context of the Ten Commandments was dictated by God, and the rest of the Old Testament proves that God was far from disapproving of all killing. God is shown very often countenancing and helping, even commanding, the wars waged by Israel. "He teacheth my hands to war and my fingers to fight," a Psalmist says, speaking as Israel's representative.[1] Sometimes God is spoken of as Himself taking part in battle, as the national War-god—"Yahweh is a man of war: Yahweh is his name."[2] "Yahweh strong and mighty, Yahweh mighty in battle."[3] On occasion He commanded the slaughter of whole tribes, such as the Amalekites, and the king of the Amalekites the prophet Samuel, acting as God's minister, "hacked to pieces before the Lord." When Phinehas found a man of Israel consorting with a Midianite woman, Phinehas took a javelin and "thrust both of them through, the man of Israel, and the woman through her belly."[4] God expresses signal approbation of the action. Now, when a Modernist is confronted with these things in the Old Testament he is not disconcerted. He says, "Yes, of course, much in the Old Testament is on a lower level of religious apprehension: we need not suppose that when God is described as approving of the action of Phinehas, the character of God, as we know it now, is revealed." It would therefore be open to a Modernist to hold that the killing of man by man is always dis-

[1] Psalm cxliv. 1.
[2] Exodus xv. 3.
[3] Psalm xxiv. 8.
[4] Numbers xxv. 8.

pleasing to God, and he can dismiss the passages in the Old Testament in which God approves of killing, as, to that extent, untrue. But a Fundamentalist cannot possibly take this line. All those Old Testament passages which ascribe to God approval of war and killing, were, he holds, dictated by God Himself and are of as unquestionable authority as the Ten Commandments. For him the Sixth Commandment cannot mean that God disapproves of all killing: it can only mean that He disapproves of what we call "murder"—that is, unauthorized killing.[1] On the other hand, a Modernist, with his view of the Old Testament, cannot accept the story of the giving of the Law as a strictly historical account of something that really happened. He does not believe that God really wrote ten commandments on two tablets of stone, and the prohibitions in the Ten Commandments have for him Divine authority only in so far as the religious and ethical ideas at which Israel had arrived when the story was written have been confirmed in the subsequent experience of Israel and of the Christian society. If the Modernist happens to be also a pacifist, he will say of course that the killing of man by man is always displeasing to God, but he will not be able to base that view upon an acceptance of the Ten Commandments as literally dictated by God. The argument, therefore, that Christians must not kill in war because one of the Ten Commandments is an unqualified prohibition of committing murder implies that you take of a particular passage in the Old Testament a view similar to the Fundamentalist one, and a Modernist view of the rest of the Old Testament.

[1] As a matter of fact, the Hebrew word used does mean "murder," not killing in general: it is used only of the killing of man by man in private quarrels, never of killing by soldiers in battle.

It is strange that anyone can reflect for five minutes without seeing the absurdity of this.

One way by which some pacifists try to get out of the absurdity is by saying that they do not regard the command " Thou shalt not kill " as Divinely given because it is one of the Ten Commandments promulgated by the God of the Hebrews, but because it was laid down by Jesus when He spoke to the rich young man. But Jesus cited the commandment " Thou shalt do no murder " from the Old Testament. He did not intimate that He was laying down any new commandment. In its Old Testament context the commandment, as we have just seen, could not possibly have meant that all taking of life was displeasing to God, but only unauthorized killing, murder. If Jesus had put an extended sense upon the commandment, when He quoted it, a sense incompatible with its Old Testament context, He would have spoken falsely. For He said to the young man " Thou knowest the commandments." It is safe to say that the young man did not know, either in the Old Testament or in the Jewish tradition, any commandment which meant " Thou shalt not in any circumstances take life." When, in the Sermon on the Mount, Jesus cites some of the old commandments with extensions made on His own authority, He does not say " Ye have heard that it was said to them of old time ' Thou shalt do no murder,' but I say unto you, Kill not at all, neither by judgment, because the judge of flesh and blood beareth not the sword of God, neither in battle, because ye owe no service to the kingdoms of this world." He said something quite different, " Whosoever is angry with his brother is in danger of the judgment." To say that a command of Christ forbidding His followers to take part in war can be constructively inferred from some of His sayings—

"Resist not evil" and so on—is one thing: to say that there is any command of Christ expressly saying "Thou shalt not in any circumstances take life" is another thing, and untrue. There is no such command.

There is indeed one form of pacifism for which I think a better case can be made out—one might call it contingent pacifism. This would be compatible with a recognition that war in the past has sometimes served a useful purpose, that on those occasions it did more good than harm, and that Christians—Joan of Arc, for instance—rightly engaged in war as a service rendered to God. It would be free from such nonsense as that force never settles anything. But it would hold that war such as it has come to be under present conditions must do more harm than good. There are circumstances in which it is the lesser evil to allow the bully to have his way. Suppose a number of people are escaping from a shipwreck in a crowded boat and one of them displays a propensity to play the bully, it might capsize the boat and drown the whole company to oppose him by force. It might be prudent in such circumstances for others in the boat not to offer that forcible resistance to the bully which they would rightly offer if they were all on dry land. Circumstances in the world to-day, it might be urged, are analogous. We are all in a position of such precarious balance that war may bring the whole of civilization to a crash. It is preferable, therefore, to suffer even the worst that the aggressive and bullying Power can do rather than oppose it by arms. Many of the arguments used against ordinary pacifism are inapplicable to such contingent pacifism. If it honestly calculates all the consequences of the bully's having his way and nevertheless maintains that the consequences of war under present conditions are worse, the contention would not be easy to overthrow. The chief reason for rejecting it is, I think, that where we see freedom-loving peoples to-day subjected to the actual experience of modern war with all its horrors they do not appear to find the horrors so great that they think submission to the enemy preferable. The Chinese and the Finns are still at the time I write this holding out with unbroken resolution; the Poles endured unspeakable horrors before they were beaten to the ground. And the judgment of the world regards such resistance not as a regrettable folly, but as admirable and heroic. We should not have thought better of the Chinese if they had given way to the Japanese without a struggle, or of the Finns if they had given way to the Russians. Their estimate of the worth of freedom is as high as that; it would be hard for any of us to say that they are wrong; and they do not have to calculate the evils of war as a future possibility; they might then be suspected of having made them too light in the reckoning; they experience them already. Thus their example weighs heavily against the contingent pacifism which alleges that the evils of war under modern conditions are so great that it is preferable to surrender to the bully. Yet it is conceivable that a state of the world might come when such contingent pacifism would be right, when the evils of war really would be greater than the evils of surrender.

The most unreasonable attitude of all is that of the people who, without being themselves pacifists, sneer at the ministers of the Christian Church, because they have encouraged men to take up military service and go into the battle. For a Quaker, of course, it is perfectly consistent to condemn Christian ministers who do this, because Quakers believe that such

L

ministers are acting against the teaching of Christ. But for anybody who is not prepared to say that a man who engages in war always does wrong—that the Finns, for instance, are doing wrong in fighting against the Russian aggressor—it shows a singularly warped mind to blame Christian ministers for giving encouragement and spiritual comfort to those who face the ordeal of war, when to face that ordeal is their duty. There are critics of the Church who seem to think that, while it is sometimes right for men to engage in war, all that the Church should do for them when they go forth is to wring its hands and lament over them and say that it is all horrible. If it does anything else than that, they say that the Church has grievously discredited its Christian profession. The fact probably is that they dislike the Church and so are glad to seize any occasion of throwing stones at it, without considering what self-stultifications they may involve themselves in, when they do so.

CHAPTER IX

WHAT OUGHT WE TO DO?

Enough has now been said about pacifism for the purpose of this book. We come then to the position of the great majority of British Christians, confronted with this war. There is general agreement that the British Commonwealth, in alliance with France, is right in exerting itself to the full extent of its resources in order to make Nazi Germany restore complete freedom to the peoples it has crushed and give them back their territory. So long as the war lasts, the question, What ought Christians to do about it? What overt practical action ought they to take? is capable of a simple answer. They ought to do anything they can to hasten the defeat of the Nazi *régime*. The problem arises in regard to the world settlement which they ought to have in view when the war is won. And by the manner in which you conceive of that settlement, your pronouncements of intention, to-day, while the war is going on, are affected, and public pronouncements may to some extent determine the course things take, by the reaction to them of people in Germany, and in other countries.

What ought we to do, when the victory is won? The important thing to make clear first, when you discuss this question, is whom do you mean by " we "? You may mean the people of all nations, or of all the nations concerned, and the question then means,

Suppose all peoples—or all European peoples—had the right will, how would international relations be ordered? Here again, the answer, from the Christian point of view, is fairly simple. Every group which desired to live as a distinct nation would have complete freedom to do so and enjoy the territory belonging to it. There would be no enmity between nations: the small ones would be as secure as the great, because no one would desire to make them afraid. Each people would recognize fraternity and preserve fellowship with all others, and none would seek to grasp more than its due share of the good things of the world. In matters of the mind and spirit there would be complete liberty of exchange across all frontiers, so that in this respect the world would be a single society enjoying its spiritual and artistic products in common. For objects of common concern the leading men of all peoples would consult together and arrange co-operative action. Suppose by reason of the growth or decrease of population in any particular area, a readjustment of the territorial distribution was, later on, called for, such readjustment would be carried out in an amicable way by general conference. There could be no war, because no people would want to attack another. And because there could be no war, there would be no need for any defensive armaments: armies and navies would have been abolished: there would be no need for any coercive League of Nations.

That is what we men, we Europeans, would do if we were all good and wise. How easy it is, sitting in our chair, to throw out freehandedly the fashion and figure of the world as it ought to be! But the answer to the question, What ought we to do? if we give "we" this large extension, does not help much to show the next step which "we," in a narrower sense, ought to take. That ideal state of the world presupposes the complete elimination of the evil will, and we have no reason to expect the miracle which would eliminate the evil will in any near future. True, an imagination of the ideal world may, even so, not be useless. To some extent we can act even now, our own nation can act even now, in the spirit of that world—we can recognize fraternity and preserve fellowship individually with men of other nations; our own nation may abstain from grabbing more than its fair share of the good things of the earth and from using its power for oppressive domination, and we may individually do our own small part to create the public opinion which will influence the Government's policy in the right way. But if we ask the question, What ought we to do? for the purpose of action now or to-morrow or next year, " we " must have a smaller extension. One must take it for granted that the evil will continues to operate in the world, that particular groups or nations may be actuated by it. Our " we " will then exclude such groups or nations, and the question will mean, Suppose a certain part of mankind, or of European mankind, is likely to be actuated by an evil will of aggression, what are we, the peaceably-minded part of mankind to do about it? Or we may give the " we " a more restricted sense and mean, What are we, the people of the British Commonwealth, to do about it? Or, in a more restricted sense still, What are we, who want to follow Christian principles, to do about it, supposing our own nation shows signs of being swayed by the evil will? It will be seen that very different answers may be given to the question, " What ought we to do? " according to the extension you give to " we," and I think a great deal of discussion to-day is confused and unprofitable just because people try to answer the question without first fixing clearly what " we " they have in mind.

All schemes of collective defence, whether that of the League of Nations or those based on the idea of Federation, which is now in the ascendant, proceed on the supposition that some nation or some nations may be actuated by the evil will. The principle of these schemes is that the other nations, or a *bloc* of other nations, should bind themselves together and unite their forces in defence of any member of the *bloc* which may be threatened by the aggressive nation. Now it is obviously important to determine in regard to any such scheme what proportion you expect the aggressive Power or Powers to bear to the peaceable Powers. The supposition which the framers of the League of Nations had in view was that any aggressor in the future was likely to possess so small an aggregate of power, as against the united strength of peaceable powers forming the League, that he would have no chance at all, and could be crushed fairly easily, none of the smaller states in the League running any great risks by taking part in the collective effort. All the members of the League might have a comfortable sense of real security, collective security. If this expectation had proved correct, the system of the League might have worked effectually. The reason the League broke down was that the Powers actuated by the evil will proved to form so large a bulk that an attempt of the peaceable Powers of the League to coerce them, instead of being an easy job involving no great risks, would have meant a sanguinary war with very great risks and probably immense loss of lives and treasure. When that happened, it was all up with collective *security*, though there was still a possibility of collective defence.

It is no doubt possible to look for the causes of the

League's breakdown further back. The reason, it may be said, why certain Powers conceived aggressive designs was that the League did not use its machinery (Article 19) to effect changes in the existing status by peaceable arrangement, it stood for a rigid maintenance of that status, favourable to Britain and France, and so drove the dissatisfied Powers to resort to violence, as the only way to remedy the injustices under which they suffered. This opens large questions—how far the dissatisfied Powers had real ground for feeling present arrangements to be unfair to them, and, if so, what could have been done to remove their grievances in a way which was not unfair to other peoples, to Czechs and Poles and Abyssinians or to the black peoples of Africa? To discuss these questions is outside the scope of this book. Whatever excuse there may, or may not, have been for three major Powers—Japan, Italy and Germany—becoming aggressive, as soon as they did become aggressive, they could not be checked by the peaceable Powers of the League, except by a war of incalculable dimensions. Does anybody still suppose you could have done it by "sanctions" without war?

And there was another essential consideration, overlooked by most of those who put their trust in the League. The difference of geographical position occupied on the globe by the nations composing the League made the League theory inapplicable. It was very easy to put down on paper the populations and military resources of the League states, great and small, and show that when you added them all up together the total was greater than the population and military resources of Japan or Italy or Germany. But, if it came to practice, the geographical position of the different League states would make the burdens they would have each to incur, in the event of war, very unequal. The first signal failure of the League to stop an aggressor was when Japan possessed itself of Manchuria. But if the League had proceeded to warlike action, it was upon one state alone that the burden of war would have fallen, upon Great Britain, with some help perhaps to be expected from the French Navy. It was no good reckoning up the armaments possessed by other League states; their geographical position in Europe made it impossible for those armaments to come into action in the Pacific. Thus what would have been called "collective security" would, in this case, have meant, as a matter of fact, a duel between Great Britain and Japan, in which Britain would have fought at a disadvantage owing to its distance from its base, while the situation in Europe made it exceedingly dangerous for Britain to send a large proportion of its Navy so far away. Or take the problem of stopping Germany by collective League action. The smaller states conterminous with Germany would be exposed, if they took up an attitude hostile to Germany, to immense dangers from which the states farther away would be free. They might be overrun and struck down by Germany before the collective strength of the other League states could be brought to bear, and even if Germany were defeated in the end, the smaller state might be left ravaged and destroyed, with a good part of its population killed. No wonder that a small state in such a geographical position thinks twice before combining with other League states to impose sanctions.

We do not know—that is the most important consideration—what kind of Germany we shall have to deal with, if Germany is defeated. When our Government says that it has no intention to destroy Germany, that it is fighting against the Nazi *régime*, not against the German people, someone will start up to tell you that to make a distinction between the German Government and the German people is absurd. The German Government is solidly supported by the people. Both are equally bad. Every nation has the Government it deserves. It is idle to suppose that the German people will be any less aggressive in temper in days to come than it has been hitherto: "the leopard cannot change his spots." We shall have to reckon with the existence in the centre of Europe of a people permanently on the look-out, whenever opportunity offers, to prey upon its neighbours. To come to any amicable arrangement with Germany which we could trust Germany to observe is utterly impossible: the only thing to do is to remain always and for ever sufficiently armed to hold Germany down by sheer force, prevent Germany from ever again building up a military force which can menace the world.

Now it is, of course, perfectly true that at the present moment we are fighting German armies recruited from the mass of the people, as well as the Nazi Government, and that the Nazi Government can still induce millions of Germans to work for it and support its Army and Navy by the taxes they pay. But it is not true that all the people desire the Nazi *régime* to go on: by very large numbers Hitler and his *régime* are hated. It is not true that in the past the aggressive elements, the spotted leopards, in Germany have been co-extensive with the people. There have always been civilized Liberal anti-militarist elements opposed to the militarists, and it is these elements who have contributed the greatest names to German literature. In the small states, which existed before the Reich was founded by Bismarck, Liberal elements often had great influence. We have, therefore, to distinguish in past history three elements

—the militarist set, the Liberal opposition, and the mass of the people who were neither militarist nor definitely anti-militarist, but accepted with little criticism the views instilled into them by the Government and marched with docility when a militarist Government ordered them to march. Under the Nazi *régime* the Liberal and anti-militarist elements have been crushed as they have never been crushed before. When a Government rests upon the free consent of the people it is fair to say that that people has the Government it deserves. But it is quite unfair to say this of the German people to-day. Its better elements are being held down by the Nazi gang who has seized the central power, held down by terror and torture. Thousands are in concentration camps. It is easy to say that if the Liberal Germans were braver, they would have got rid of this *régime*. With modern scientific means of destruction, of detection and communication, a gang in possession of the central power can extinguish instantly any individual who dares to raise his head in criticism, long before any opposition can be organized. I do not know how many of us would be brave if bravery meant being put to torture in a concentration camp. Because the Liberal elements are suppressed and muzzled, we do not know yet how large a proportion of the people, if the iron hand were removed, they would prove to be.

Thus, if we hope for a better Germany in days to come, with which we can have normal dealings, it is not that we expect any leopards to change their spots; what we hope is that the better elements now suppressed by force, elements who are not spotted, will come to have the direction of things, that the mass of the people will be as docile to a Liberal Government as they have been to militarist ones, and that the leopards, if they remain as darkly spotted as ever, will have lost their power to rule the State. It seemed as if this had happened in the early days of the Republic at the end of 1918. A wave of vehement anti-militarism swept through the German people, a revulsion from the war. Officers who appeared in the streets in uniform were set upon by the multitude and had their shoulder straps cut off. I was seeing at that time people who had come from Germany. They agreed in saying that in the present mood of the German people, their disgust with the rulers now overthrown, their sense of bewilderment, their readiness to accept any friendly hand held out by the English to guide them, "you could do absolutely anything you like with them." That the militarist set soon got back again into the saddle, is largely due to England's failing to hold out the friendly hand. It is not the crank of a few soft-headed people to say that at that moment we treated the Germans unwisely and ungenerously. It has been said by Mr. Neville Chamberlain.

We do not know what will happen in Germany if Hitler and his gang are overthrown. The Liberal elements presumably will come forth into the open from the concentration camps and the homes where all these years they have kept a terrified silence, and maybe a large proportion of the people will rally to their call. But there will now be a complication in the thousands of ferocious young leopards who have grown up under the Nazi *régime* and been trained to admire violence and domineering and cruelty. Probably the Liberal elements consist mainly of the older people. What is to be done with these hordes of savage young men? They cannot be annihilated: it is questionable how far they can now be brought to a better mind. How will they ever be fitted, as decent, quiet workers, into the frame of a Liberal Germany?

If the Liberal elements take it in hand to suppress them that may mean sanguinary fighting. It may be that in the civil war large numbers of them will be killed, and the problem in that way become less insoluble.

It is likely that the leopard elements will be in the minority, and that the large bulk of the people will turn upon the overthrown rulers, as they did at the end of 1918. I have seen a forecast by a German refugee in this country, not a Jew nor a Communist, but an Aryan and a Liberal, a man whose opinion, from his previous work in Germany, is to be respected. He rejoices, in anticipation, to see the vengeance, horrible as he thinks it will be, very much as Tertullian exulted to think of the pains the persecutors would suffer in hell. But he is convinced that after there has been this great purge the aggressively-minded elements in Germany will have been thrown from power and the evil spirit which dominated Germany so often in the past will be cast out for good.

Yes, the train of events, once set in motion, may well take a course at which we shall have to look on, with little power to control. It seems *naïf* to sit down now and plot out our designs for the new world after the war, as if the world would be passive material which we shall be able to fashion to our desire. We can only bear witness to the ideal and adapt the real world to the ideal, when the time comes, so far as circumstances allow. No doubt to go on bearing witness to the ideal, through good and evil days, is just one of the things that Christians are here in the world to do, and in the long run the actual course of things may be affected by that witness. Perhaps, for that very reason, Christians are liable to avert their eyes from awkward facts of the real world. We can say in a moment what, in accordance with the ideal, we desire the future relations of the British people and the German people to be. We desire that, transcending the national difference, there should be fellowship between the two nations as members of the one human family, that we should rejoice to see a prosperous, happy, spiritually productive Germany, that Germany should have to suffer nothing incompatible with its proper dignity as a nation, that there should be free and frequent intercourse between individual Englishmen and individual Germans, that we should communicate to each other our spiritual, intellectual, artistic good things.

We can keep that ideal in view, whatever kind of Germany emerges from the war. But till we know what kind of Germany does emerge, we cannot know how far reality can be conformed in our own time to the ideal. If the German Liberal to whom I referred just now is right, we shall have, after some scenes of horror, a Germany in which militarism is suppressed for good. Then the problem of coming to terms with the new Germany will be simple. Whether the European states federate or not, there will be no great need for federation, because the danger from German aggressiveness will have ceased. On the other hand, if there is still a Germany there in which aggressively-minded elements have the direction, the problem of defence for the other European states will be grave.

Perhaps the way in which such a situation might most easily come about is a compromise peace. When the course of the war makes the pressure on Germany more severe, the Nazis in power are almost certain to make peace proposals which go further than anything they are willing to concede at present, but do not go far enough to bring about their downfall. They would offer, perhaps, to withdraw their armies from Czechoslovakia and Poland and concede these countries a kind of autonomy which would still leave them at Germany's mercy, still virtually client-states. If that happens it is natural that many people in England should ask whether it is really worth the strain and the losses of further months or years of war simply to secure the margin between what the Germans offer and a full restoration of the subjugated peoples. There will be a temptation to agree to a compromise which would leave a Nazi Government in power. By such a compromise we should, it is quite true, obtain immediate relief. But the situation with which we should then be faced in the coming years would be fearful. We should see no end to the strain of always remaining alert and heavily armed to meet a new aggression. One ground for believing that we shall avoid the danger of agreeing to such a compromise is that our French allies are determined to go on fighting this time till the German danger is removed, and it would involve breaking with them to agree to unsatisfactory proposals of peace.

Yet we cannot be quite sure that, even if Germany is defeated, even if this *régime* is overthrown, the spotted leopards in Germany may not again get control of the State. It is a possibility with which we have to reckon that Germany may still be dangerous. Faced with such a position of affairs, British Christians, if they are going to indicate what they believe to be the right course, will have to choose between one of two lines of action. Either they will have to take the pacifist position and say that the British Government ought to allow Germany to carry out its will upon the world, opposing aggression by no more than verbal protests and remonstrances, or they will have to give their approval and support to measures taken by the British Government to maintain permanently an armed strength superior to Germany's.

Let us suppose they choose the second of these alternatives. The superiority of the armed strength opposed to Germany's may be brought about in one of two different ways—by making Germany weak or by making ourselves enormously strong. The recommendation of the first way of doing it would be that it would save us the frightful strain of keeping up huge armaments and perpetual readiness for war. It could probably be done if Germany's defeat were decisive. There is, I believe, a considerable section of French opinion which holds that the only course which would bring security and relief to Europe in time to come, is to break up the German Reich into separate states, attaching Catholic Bavaria perhaps to Catholic Austria, and isolating Prussia. Some circles here are shocked at such proposals as wicked, as inflicting real injustice upon the German people. They certainly would be wicked, if we have any ground after the war for believing that the peaceably-minded elements in Germany have come into control. But, if we have not, if Germany is still ruled by elements who are waiting for an opportunity to threaten Europe, and if we, on our side, have made up our mind that superiority of strength is to be secured somehow or other to the Powers which stand for freedom, I do not see that it is more wicked to bring about Germany's inferiority by breaking up Germany than by confronting a strong Germany with a still greater aggregate of power, an aggregate so great as to prevent Germany by a rigid bar from achieving its desire. It is not a normal act of love to my neighbour to compel him to wear a strait waistcoat, but, if my neighbour happens to be a dangerous maniac, it may be justifiable to do so. If Germany were rendered so weak that the other nations could enjoy security without the continuous strain of keeping up immense armaments, it would be better for the world generally than if such a strain has to be endured. I do not therefore think that on moral grounds we can repudiate such a procedure as one which we ought in no circumstances to entertain.

Yet there are great objections to this course. If the Germans want to form a single state, then to break up the people politically, while it would make it more difficult for them to act together in the very near future, would greatly inflame their desire to go to war again later on. It would not be so easy to keep the German states apart, if they wished to act together. It would be just as difficult as it would be to break up the British Commonwealth, if its nations wished to act together. Suppose you detached Canada and Australia as independent states, how could you prevent them shaping their politics in concert with Great Britain, if they were free to do as they chose? To keep the German states separated against their will might, in the end, involve as great a military strain for Britain and France, as to coerce a united Germany. And one must remember that there are many intermediate degrees between a Germany wholly set on future war and a Germany determined to keep the peace. There would be large elements in the country more or less uncertain, who might be swayed one way or the other according to circumstances, and to inflict upon Germany what all these people would feel to be intolerable injustice would be to exasperate these elements, and cause them to throw themselves on the side of the militarists. Again, if we disclosed now any intention to break up Germany it would prolong the present war. Large numbers of Germans who dislike the present *régime* and would be ready, if the war begins obviously to go badly, to overthrow it and agree to reasonable terms of peace, would support the Nazi Government in continuing the fight, if they thought surrender meant the break-up of Germany. It is one of the most effective strokes in the Nazi Government's home propaganda to tell the German people over and over again that Britain and France are out to disintegrate the Reich, and any utterances on this side which tend to confirm such a statement cause the anti-Nazi Germans who have found a refuge abroad to wring their hands.

A less objectionable way of securing that, although with only moderate armaments, we still had a decisive military superiority over Germany would be to prevent Germany from having armaments above a certain figure. That, of course, was done, as a temporary measure, after the last war. The restriction might be maintained much longer, as long indeed as the spirit dominant in Germany was such as to cause mistrust. No doubt, there would, in such a case, be a certain amount of secret rearming, but if the inspectors appointed by the other nations were vigilant, the more formidable instruments of war could not be manufactured on a large scale without being detected. It may be said that such control would be felt by Germans to be just as grave a humiliation as a division of their country, and that it would therefore be open to the same objection: it would keep alive in many Germans, who might otherwise have been peaceably-minded, a fierce resolve to renew the fight. Perhaps the effect of armament-control might be neutralized if in other ways Germany were treated with consideration and if continued experience convinced the Germans that the other nations did not want to use their superiority of power to put Germany at any disadvantage in respect of economic facilities or internal freedom, that Germany, even if unable to seize its fair share of the goods of the world by armed force, could securely enjoy its fair share by the good-will of the other nations. If the victors in 1918 had been sagacious they would, I think, have set two main objects before themselves in the treatment of Germany: they would, on the one hand, have arranged that the new republican Germany should enjoy the maximum of economic comfort, that in international dealings it should be accorded all the forms of respect, and that its cultural achievements should have warm recognition in other countries—that the Germans should be treated, in a word, in such a way that their present condition should seem to them preferable to their condition under the *régime* of William II. If this meant that the victorious Allies forwent reparations, a sacrifice which secured a contented Germany would have saved them the expenditure entailed by another war, or entailed by armaments piled up in the fear of another war. On the other hand, the Allies should have been adamant in not permitting Germany to rearm. What we actually did was in each respect the opposite; we treated Germany, on the one hand, in such a way that the Germans did look back to the Hohenzollern *régime* with regret, in contrast with the distressful and humiliating present, and, on the other hand, we allowed Germany to re-arm. We were too rigorous in inflicting hard conditions upon them by way of punishment, and we were too easy-going and weak-handed in control in regard to the secret rearming under the Republic; and when Germany became truculent under the Nazi *régime* and openly began to rearm, we ceased to offer any opposition to Hitler's rebuilding a strong military power, although in the early stages of the Nazi *régime* we might have stopped this quite easily.

For the strange paralysis which marked British and French policy in regard to Germany in the years 1933 to 1937, we are having to make up fearfully to-day.

One way then of securing a superiority of strength on the side of the anti-Nazi states, suppose after the war the spotted leopards in Germany regain control, is to prevent the reconstitution of a German military power. The other way is to amass a greater aggregate of military power on our side. If we prove unable to prevent Germany making itself strong again, to maintain a superior strength permanently on our side would, as has been indicated, entail a strain which is fearful to contemplate and which in the long run our people might not endure. People who tell us that this is what we have got to do, do not seem to realize what an appalling prospect they set before us. That is why so many people to-day seek a solution of the problem in Federation. Britain and France would not need, they think, to maintain these tremendous armaments, because they would form a political union with a number of other states, whose united armaments, although separately they may be minor Powers, would, if added to relatively modest armaments maintained by Britain and France, secure a preponderance of strength over Germany. Mr. Clarence Streit, of course, contemplates the United States entering into his Federation, but the general opinion is that there is no chance of the people of the United States entertaining such an idea in any future we can foresee.

There is perhaps as great a danger that people should give themselves a feeling of comfort to-day by talking about Federation as they did some years ago by talking about " collective security." Christians may be specially liable to indulge in wishful imagination about Federation because they desire to see the nations united in fellowship, and Federation seems to imply this coming about in the case of a large group of nations. We should recognize, I think, that a state of the world in which affairs of common interest to all nations, or to all the nations inhabiting some particular area, were ordered by united consultation would be a desirable state of the world, and that if any great Power shows a disposition to make war in pursuit of ambitious schemes it would be wise for all the nations who might be attacked by it to join beforehand in common defence. But if Federation in some form is our ideal, it is well that we should look squarely at the adverse facts. In the first place, it is to-day by no means clear that a Federation, even if it included the Scandinavian, the Balkan, and the Near Eastern states, would balance in numbers the tyrannic Powers. We are considering, remember, at present the problem of the future on the hypothesis that Germany continues to be dominated by a temper of aggressive ambition, but we have now to reckon with the possibility that the man-power and resources of Germany and Russia will be combined. In the present war indeed it seems doubtful whether Germans will be able to get much from Russia, but this does not rule out the possibility that in the future Germany may be able to obtain control of Russia and, creating an organization which the Russians seem temperamentally incapable of creating for themselves, present the world with a terrific accumulation of power. It may be that Japan would enter into the coalition in order to secure its domination of China. In contemplation of such a vast extension of tyrannic power from the French frontier across Asia to the Pacific little comfort can be got by murmuring the blessed word "Federation." Of course, if the Federation included India's 400,000,000, the populations included in it would outnumber those of the tyrannic Powers, but it would be idle to suppose that more than a small proportion of India's millions would furnish man-power for armies, or if we suppose armies raised in India proportionate to the population, these armies would so enormously outnumber the other military forces of the Federation, that India would dominate all the other states composing it. If, on the other hand we leave out India, the populations of the states composing the Federation, supposing these consisted of the British Commonwealth, France, Belgium, Holland, the Scandinavian countries, Portugal, Switzerland, Czechoslovakia, Poland, Hungary, Yugoslavia, Rumania, Bulgaria, Greece, Egypt, Turkey and Iraq, would do no more than approximately equal the populations of Germany and the Soviet Union, without Japan.

But let us suppose that the military forces of the Federation, if all put into the field, would greatly outnumber the forces of the tyrannic Power, there is still the difficulty already spoken of, arising from the differences of geographical position. It is continually pointed out that the formation of a Federation would imply that the states composing it renounced their separate sovereignty—" pooled their sovereignty " the phrase is—or at any rate admitted restrictions to it, and it is supposed that the clinging to their separate sovereignty from a sentiment which comes down from the past is the great obstacle which has to be surmounted. Now this sentiment is no doubt an obstacle, but I do not think the sentimental difficulty is the gravest. A greater difficulty is the unwillingness of any people to incur the sufferings and losses of war in any quarrel in which its vital interests are not immediately and obviously concerned. The difficulty would be especially great, in the case of those smaller peoples which, from their geographical position, would be exposed to the first brunt of a German attack—countries such as Belgium, Holland, or Denmark. Even if the forces of the Federation exceeded in numbers those of Germany, it might be very difficult to give any of these smaller peoples the assurance that the forces of the Federation would be assembled quickly enough to save them, should the German attack be sudden, from being overrun and devastated. Thus one could not promise them any certain protection in return for a surrender of the separate sovereignty, and they might well feel it safer to have the status of neutrals outside any such Federation. It is possible indeed that in course of time a Maginot line might be constructed along all the land-frontiers of Germany which would hold up any German aggression at whatever point it might be attempted, long enough for the superior forces of the Federation to be brought to bear. This would be an "encirclement" of Germany indeed!

Effective federation also implies that a feeling of solidarity extends through all the federated peoples such as it is hard to foresee existing in any near future. Suppose the Germans to-day effected a landing in the north of Scotland and a Devonshire regiment were among the forces sent north to deal with the invader, no grievance would be felt in Devonshire, because men of Devon are sent to fight so far away. People in Exeter would not say, "What have we to do with defending Caithness or Aberdeen?" The feeling of solidarity through the whole population of Great Britain, the growth of centuries of political union, is such that the idea of such a question being asked to-day seems absurd. But would the Swedes, in any near future, willingly see their soldiers sent away to fight and die to repel an aggression in

Rumania? Yet until Swedes feel this to be just as much a matter of course as the people of Devonshire would feel it that a Devonshire regiment should take part in the defence of Scotland, a Federation which included Sweden and Rumania could not have such solidarity as would make the union of its military resources effective. The League failed because the states composing it were not willing to engage in actual war, with all its agonies, except for the defence of their own national territory: and if we pin our hopes of a better world on the establishment of a European Federation, that too will fail, unless the states composing it are willing to go to war, even when they are not themselves threatened.

One thing is plain to-day. If great states are going to be actuated in days to come by the will to aggress, the smaller states will be sooner or later swallowed up, unless they are attached to some larger whole which will afford them collective protection. A pitiable picture is exhibited to-day by the shivering neutrals—the Scandinavian states, Denmark, Holland —who cling desperately to their neutrality, even though they try to succour their neighbour Finland, for whom they feel real and deep concern, in any ways that will not too dangerously provoke Germany or Russia. The only thing which might compel them to merge their sovereignty by joining a large federation and accepting the obligations of membership, is fear, fear of the great aggressive states. In his book *Mitteleuropa*, much read in Germany during the last war, Friedrich Naumann insisted that the day of small states was over, that only states with extensive areas and great military resources could survive under the conditions of the modern world. This is true, if big states are going to be aggressive. If no state wanted to aggress, there would be no strong reason for federation. Federation, if it comes, will be simply the response to the evil will: it is not anything good in itself. On the contrary, if the evil will were eliminated, there would be a great deal to be said for the world being divided into small sovereign states. German culture at its best was the culture of the small German states. In a small state the Government is much nearer the ordinary man of the people. They can go their own ways in their institutions, modes of life, intellectual and artistic activity, and so produce a richer variety, which would be all to the good and would make the world more interesting. If the relations of all these states were friendly, if they communicated their intellectual and artistic achievements, if the members of any one state could travel freely through the others and study their peculiarities, there would be no harm in their separate political independence. But when there are great aggressive states close by, this happy quiet life of small states is impossible. Only big states can then be secure, and it is largely in order to make sure of being able to hold their own in a warring world that states are avid to grasp more territory and accumulate more power.

Thus the question how far, when the war is over, the peaceable states will be driven to federate depends on the question how far the evil will in other nations will prevail. We do not know that, and because we do not know it, it is idle to suppose that we can at this stage enunciate our scheme for the settlement of the world after the war. We do not know what kind of Germany, what kind of Russia, what kind of Italy, we shall have to deal with. We do not know what course our French allies will think it wise to follow in regard to the Germany that is there then, whatever that Germany may be. We do not know what kind of arrangements the nations that so far are still neutral will be willing to fall in with. How can we, the British, lay down the form to be given to the new world, as if it rested with us alone to decide that? We can do no more, when the time comes, than state what, in our judgment, would be the wise thing to do: we do not know how far we shall have to adapt ourselves to the judgment of others. There is a phrase, used I think mainly in circles belonging to the Opposition in recent years, which has always seemed to me a singularly infelicitous one: we must "build up" a system of collective security or collective defence. The National Government was commonly blamed because it did not "build up" such a system. As if the other nations were inanimate blocks which the British Government could shift and pile up and arrange in any form it chose! The other nations are entities with views and wills of their own; the most we can do is to put our views before them.

All these measures, remember—breaking up Germany, keeping it disarmed, forming a federation of superior strength, surrounding it with a Maginot line—have been discussed only on the hypothesis that the eighty millions of Germans in the centre of Europe continue after this war to be governed by those elements whose will is for aggression. If this proves to be the case, I think we must frankly recognize that, whatever we do, the time before us will be a dark and terrible one, a time of continuous strain, in which the necessities of defence will absorb the money and energies that might have gone to improving social conditions and will crush out many of the amenities of life, many pleasant literary and artistic interests, which require an environment of security and peace. It may be that however reasonable and generous offers we might make to Germany, to induce it to come into some settlement of Europe which secured the freedom and peace of all, they would be quite unavailing to melt, deep down in the hearts of the rulers of Germany, after this present attempt to dominate Europe and the world has been frustrated, the hard resolve to try again. It is shallow optimism to suppose that we can always by some action of ours convert the evil will. If the evil will continues to dominate Germany (and Russia) there may be nothing we can do, nothing at all, to change it. And if it is not changed, nothing we do can prevent the coming time from being grievous. All that Christians can say in such a case is that in unnumbered individual lives on earth God allows long stretches of distress and pain, and that in the past He has sometimes allowed long stretches of distress and pain to occur in the lives of peoples. For all we know, it may be His will that the world during the next generations should go through a period of distress and pain. If so, there is nothing in that to overthrow a Christian's faith. He must have recognized long ago that distress and pain, assigned in whatever measure God sees best, belong to this world of probation. He must bear the pain and distress which he shares with the world at large just as he bears the pain and distress which befall him individually, in patience and confidence that beyond the darkness there is "the inheritance incorruptible and undefiled and that fadeth not away, reserved in heaven,"[1] the union of the Divine Community in a perfection of fellowship impossible under earthly conditions. He must believe that God, who determines the particular set of conditions which constitute for each individual person the problems with which, during his passage through this world, he has to deal, sees that for the persons whose lot is cast in such a time of world-darkness, the diffi-

[1] 1 Peter i. 4.

cult conditions are those which will best form their special characters, if they deal with them rightly, for the place they are ultimately to fill in the Divine Community. The conditions will be in themselves evil, whereas the conditions of a time in which peace and freedom are secure are in themselves good, and it will be right for Christians to pray for peace and freedom, as for other good things, which God may see it best for them, during the time of their probation, to be denied, but which He may see it good that they should have, if their attitude to Him is one of trust—"Almighty and everlasting God, who dost govern all things in heaven and earth, mercifully hear the supplications of thy people, and grant thy peace to our times."[1]

Happily, the supposition that the aggressively-minded elements in Germany will continue to dominate the German people after this war is ended may not be realized. There is nothing to exclude a hope that we may have a new Germany and that the evil spirit which has ruled it in these later days will be cast out or suppressed. It is quite certain that the better elements are there, weak as they have been in the past, and crushed as they are to-day. We have seen what those Germans who, because they are opposed to the Nazi *régime*, have taken refuge abroad believe will happen if Germany is defeated again. Of course, something must be discounted in the opinions of refugees. "I know," says the line of a Greek

[1] "Omnipotens sempiterne Deus, qui coelestia simul et terrestria moderaris, supplicationes populi tui clementer exaudi, et pacem tuam nostris concede temporibus." Collect for the Second Sunday after Epiphany. Our Prayer Book translates "grant us thy peace all the days of our life," but this is to change into a petition for individual good what is, in the Latin, a petition for the good of the contemporary world—"nostra *tempora*" in the plural means what "our times" in English means.

dramatist, "that men in exile feed on hopes."[1] Yet it may be that in this case the exiles' hopes will be justified by the event. If they are, if we do have a Germany to deal with such as they forecast, none of these measures discussed just now for confining an aggressively-minded Germany within bounds would be required. We should have no cause for fear because the eighty or ninety millions of Germans formed a single state in the centre of Europe. Disarmament would no longer be encompassed with insuperable difficulties. True, if there is an aggressively-minded Russia, Europe might still have to remain armed in self-defence, but in regard to Russia too there is some hope that the elements opposed to Stalin and the ruling gang may assert themselves. It is certain that in Russia, as in Germany, there is widespread discontent. One reason alleged for Stalin's embarking on his policy of aggressive expansion is that the internal situation was so strained. This may well be true. Even then in regard to the Russia of the future we may have hope.

Christians should go to meet the coming days, whatever they may be, without fear. They can do their part strenuously and confidently in this troubled world just because the anchor of their hope is in another world, "within the veil,"[2] and they know that the ultimate future, whether beyond this sphere of things or here on earth as well, will bring full satisfaction to those who desire to see "the kingdoms of this world become the kingdom of our Lord and His Christ."[3]

[1] Æschylus, *Agamemnon*, 1668.
[2] Hebrews vi. 19. [3] Revelation xi. 15.